Wealthy Women

Wealthy Women

The Successful Woman's Guide to Real Estate Investing

Jane Fowler

Carol Wilson

Lynda Logan Frank

REGENCY BOOKS · PUBLISHERS

Designed by Christine Swirnoff / Libra Graphics, Inc.

Library of Congress Cataloging in Publication Data

Fowler, Jane.
  Wealthy women.

  1. Real estate investment. 2. Women in real estate.
I. Wilson, Carol. II Frank, Lynda Logan. III. Title.
HD1382.5.F69   1985 332.63′24′024042   85-2521
ISBN 0-910019-35-5

Published in the United States by Regency Books
                              P.O. Box 27368
                              Tempe, AZ 85282

Printed in the U.S.A.   First Edition

10   9   8   7   6   5   4   3   2

Acknowledgments

We would like to thank several people for making this book possible. Our deepest thanks to Rebecca Dickson for helping us to write and edit the book, and to our editor, Bruce Erb. We would also like to thank our publisher, Regency Books.

We would not be writing this book on investing were it not for some people whom we may not actually know personally, but whose ideas and inspiration led us to buying homes as a career. To Wade Cook, Al Lowry, Robert Allen, Mark Haroldson and all the other investors and teachers who motivated us to try something new, we send our thanks.

And finally, we would like to acknowledge all those people who intimated or told us that what we have done as three women couldn't be done by three women. Your doubts in us made us more determined— we hope you enjoy our book.

Dedicated to our husbands and children,
without whose patience, support and assistance,
our tasks would have been much more difficult.

Contents

Preface

Women have been investing in real estate for a long time, not just as real estate agents but as "down in the trenches, negotiate the deal, collect the rent" investors. Now comes a book full of hope, techniques, and "how to's" to get any woman going into this lucrative career from women who have done it very successfully.

It's not just their excitement for real estate that these authors are trying to convey; it's "here's how we did it—you can too." Any book that's going to make it has to capture this "how to" essence and this is done so, quite remarkably, here.

Real estate is used to build cash flow, or more monthly income. It's also great for tax write-offs and tax-sheltered growth. And down the road a person will have equity both from loan reduction and from appreciation, either from sweat equity or the economy in general. These are good reasons to get started, but when the reader discovers that it's probably the only investment where you can get cash flow, tax write-offs, *and* growth with the same investment dollar, and a highly leveraged dollar at that, she or he too, will get excited.

After writing my book, *How To Build A Real Estate Money Machine* and now that *Real Wealth* has hit the bookstores, the mail started and has kept coming in. About three years ago, I noticed that most of the mail was from women. More than ever, women are realizing not only their potential, but their actual abilities to convert dreams into hands-off monthly income, and to see tax-savings and assets growing that they've never thought possible.

On one of my many trips I met Lynda, Jane and Carol, and talked with them about a book. Their talent and enthusiasm is contagious. They know what they're doing, and it's not only appropriate and long overdue, but exciting to see their story in print. This is a spare-time or full-time creation of a portfolio that will stand the test of time.

I strongly encourage you to read, ponder and then go out and do what they are writing about. Real estate is an "actionable" investment and now, with this book, it will be brought within the reach of millions more.

Wade B. Cook, author of
Real Wealth and *How to Build
A Real Estate Money Machine*

11

Introduction

It's 7:35 in the morning. You smell toast burning as you stand in the bathroom, trying to force a shirt over your four-year-old's head. He is crying loudly, protesting that he doesn't want to go to school today. Your eight-year-old walks by—she looks pale and is moaning that she either has the measles or malaria. Your teenager complains that she has no clean clothes—she asks you why you never do the laundry. You yell back that you never have the time!

You're running late today. You are supposed to be at work by 8:00 and you have three breakfasts to fix and force down the throats of your kids, a child to drop off at the child-care center, two others to drop off at the bus stop, a dog to find, and a cat to feed. Work is fifteen minutes away.

Things aren't going well.

Sound familiar? Whether you have kids or not, as you're rushing around to meet an unbending early morning deadline, things can go sour. Wouldn't it be nice if you didn't have a boss to report to? Wouldn't it be great if you were doing something self-fulfilling that paid well? Wouldn't it be terrific to spend more time with those you love? And wouldn't it be absolutely heavenly to simply give up on days that start out badly and go back to sleep until, say, 11:00, when things might stand a better chance of going well?

Ladies, this is not just a dream. There is a method within your reach that will give you a life like this. From the title of this book you probably already have a clue as to what it is: real estate investments.

Does this sound like an impossible career for a woman? In the past it might have been. Women rarely worked out of the home, and, unless she had the cash in hand, a woman found it extremely difficult to buy a house. She never dreamed of even applying for a loan, because she knew she wouldn't get it.

But we women have come a long way. Women work. Women go to college. Women have careers. Women, if they have to, raise families on their own. And women now do not find it impossible to buy a home. . .or *homes*.

Many men have become investors and have proven that there is a wealthy life-style to be found via real estate investments. They have started out slowly, buying one house at a time, often while working another job. They've soon found that investing is more profitable than their eight to five jobs. And not being dummies, they quit those eight to five jobs. They leave their bosses, their rigid schedules, and deadly dull and unchanging paychecks behind forever. And they go on to find out what financial success is all about.

There is nothing to keep women from doing the same. Sure, not many have done it. But in every bank lobby or loan office, there is a sign saying the same thing: The financial institution avows that it cannot and will not reject a person applying for a loan on the basis of religion, race, color or sex. Salesmen and homeowners anywhere will treat you just as they would a male buyer: with courtesy and hope. They want to sell a house, and it makes little difference that the buyer doesn't speak with a deep voice. An offer is an offer—a seller will jump at it if it satisfies his needs.

Few women have pursued a career in real estate investing, but this is due only to the fact that few women have considered it an option. It is an option, and this book is going to show you why, and how! Take a few minutes now and do a quick evaluation of yourself.

Do you work hard? For whom or for what company do you work so strenuously? Are you happy spending your precious (and it is precious!) time this way? Are you appreciated, respected, treated well? Do you return to your home happy and satisfied, convinced that you are bringing in a good salary? If you have a husband and/or children, wouldn't you like more flexibility to deal with their needs? Is your future taken care of, either by your company or your savings account? If not, do you honestly trust Uncle Sam to make sure that you will lead the same type of life-style after you are sixty-five?

Do these questions make you look at your present employment differently? Let's try a different approach to this interrogation.

If there is anything about your present job that leaves you less than smiling, are you willing to do something about it? Are you willing to cease working for someone else and begin working hard once again, but this time for yourself? Does the idea of searching the papers, driving past properties and looking up titles in search of an ideal investment that could make you thousands of dollars sound unreasonable? Can you tolerate spending hours with a realtor, poring over an MLS and other listing books to find a good deal? Are you willing to clean and perform minor renovation of a property in order to make it sell more quickly and for a higher price?

Does this last query sound a bit much? Just how attached are you to that $14,000 per year income? (Whether you earn more or less than this is unimportant—whatever you are making, real estate investments likely will prove far more profitable.) Would you like to double or triple your income this year? Would you like to retire in five years? Maybe your present job gives you a sense of personal satisfaction, however little it provides you financially. You can keep your job and use your investments as extra income or for tax deductions. With real estate investing, you can do all of these things. It is the safest and most profitable investment around.

At this point, for you working women, perhaps we have made you ask yourself: When do I start?

We are aware, however, that many women are not working. Perhaps you are married, with or without children, and are at home most of the day. Perhaps your husband makes a great salary and you don't have to work. Would you like to save your family perhaps thousands of dollars? You can. The U.S. government has proven to be such a miserable landlord that it gives you tremendous incentive to become one yourself. This incentive is in the form of tax breaks given to owners of rental properties. By investing in rental houses, you will be bringing in additional income and at the same time getting a significant tax break. There are many real estate investors who make vast amounts of money and pay no taxes at all. How much did you pay out last year? How much will you pay out this year? Wouldn't you rather spend that money on a cruise in the Caribbean or a trip to Rio?

Or maybe your husband makes just enough for you to get by: Would you like to make your lives more comfortable? Maybe you're at home with the kids: Do you know that you can work a real estate career around children fairly easily? Your time is yours—you are your own boss. Thus, you can know the satisfaction of being there when your kids need you and yet be working at a very profitable career.

Your kids can even help. Do you remember when you were a kid and you enjoyed "helping Mommy"? Do you remember how exciting it was to paint the house? Granted, children do get bored with such tasks quickly, but then you can simply send them out to play in the backyard of your investment home. You can watch them just as if you were at home, cleaning.

With the extra money that real estate investments bring in, your life would simply be more comfortable. No worries about bills to be paid or unexpected expenses. And you could add a few luxuries. You could have lobster as often as you cared to, take a fabulous vacation, go to college, and on and on. Only your imagination limits the ways money could be used to enhance your life. And whether you are eighteen or sixty-eight, married or single, a mother or childless, college- or high-school educated, makes no difference. Even the lack of a good credit rating makes little difference—we will tell you some ways to overcome that. A successful career in real estate investing is within your capabilities. It is a viable, profitable, and creative way for you to better your present and future. All you need is ambition, knowledge, and action.

The purpose of this book is to help any woman who, for one reason or another, is not satisfied with her present financial/employment situation. First, you must overcome a formidable hurdle—the "I can't" syndrome. We hope to help you with this. In nine out of ten cases "I can't" is simply an excuse; it most certainly is an excuse when applied to the idea of women getting into real estate investing. If you want to do it, any reason for not trying has a false bottom. You have as much potential and ability (even more, in some areas) as a man does.

Most investment books are written by men. Though they might be excellent books, they can be intimidating to a woman who, perhaps, is not quite sure what equity is, let alone the rest of these new terms. Thus, since women often approach things differently than men, this book was written for and by women. Three of them, to be exact, and we three have proven that the inability to grow a beard makes no difference in making money in real estate. Can you sign your name? Can you add and subtract? Shop for bargains? And are you willing to work hard for yourself? Yes? Then you have the necessary prerequisites. We want to convince you of this and help you overcome your qualms with the idea. We will help you get started by giving you the basics and explaining our methods.

This book, however, is not intended to give the only answers to real estate investment. We did not read one book and go out and buy a home. We cautiously (and yet excitedly!) read many books—we either bought them or got them from the library (buying them is nicer—you can keep them and refer back to them). We also attended several seminars on the subject. These were not cheap, but we learned much and they were certainly worth it, whether we used a specific idea or not. It has been said many times and it applies in real estate as in all else: knowledge is power. You only stand to benefit by the discovery of new methods. (We especially recommend Wade Cook's books: *How to Build a Real Estate Money Machine, How to Pick up Foreclosures,* and *Cook's Book on Creative Financing.* Al Lowry and Robert Allen have written some good books too.)

Once we had the knowledge, we formed a partnership and bought our first property. We cleaned and remodeled it, then rented it out. We own it to this day—it still brings in a positive cash flow for us every month. We were nervous over that first buy, but it was successful and this was proof to us that, indeed, real estate investing does work. We stepped up our efforts. Today we are full-time real estate investors and far better off financially than we were before. And we have more time for ourselves and our families. If three former schoolteachers who knew little about real estate can do it, so can you.

16

Wealthy Women

CHAPTER ONE

The Ultimate Career for a Woman

A LMOST EVERYONE LIKES the idea of making more money, extra money, loads of money. Because this idea is so attractive, and because working overtime seems so unattractive, many people turn to some form of investing to add to their bank accounts. Investments are the most feasible way to wealth, and besides, they prove such a stimulating adventure! You put your money into a promising product and watch it grow, right?

Well, you hope it grows—not all investments are guaranteed money-makers. In fact, most of them entail a considerable risk to the investor. Why? Because most investments are in luxuries, and however valuable they may seem, luxuries are not so essential that the price cannot rise or drop. And not everyone wants gold, silver or other stocks. Thus, the value of those commodities fluctuates quite a bit—on a daily basis. You can never be certain that you will see your money again once you put it into such an investment. You could buy $2000 worth of stock and watch it do nothing on the market, or worse, steadily fall. It's depressing. You work hard for your money—how discouraging to watch it slowly dwindle away. In this situation you would have to sell your shares for less than what you paid for them and walk away with a lesson as your only profit.

Still, you would like to make more money than you are making now. Isn't there some investment that will bring in more money and yet allow you to sleep without worries at night? Yes, there is: real estate.

Buying real estate has proven to be the safest and most profitable investment possible. Most of the nation's millionaires got their start by buying real estate at the right time and the right price, and few of them have lost their shirts because of their investments. Why is it so safe and profitable? The answer is basic: everybody needs shelter, and real estate provides shelter. Unlike gold, silver, and stock, it is not a luxury. However important precious metals seem, they are not necessities in everyday life. Gold does look nice on one's neck and it does help support the economy, but people can exist without it. And it is not just gold that humans don't need—people can exist without just about anything found on the stock market. This does not mean that such goods are not valuable, nor does it mean they are never a good investment; it simply means they are not a certainty.

The issue comes down to supplying one of our basic needs. Just try living without a place to get a good night's sleep. How dry will a bar of gold keep you out in the wind and the rain and the snow? Not very. But real estate provides shelter, something we all need. Therefore, as an investment, it is more secure. Come what may, people will need to have a place to live.

Real estate does not go down in value: It is the only investment field that has continued to grow, whatever shape the economy is in. Only during the Great Depression did real estate values go down, and even then those values did not fall as catastrophically as other goods (and those people who managed to hold on to their property certainly did well after the depression's end—their land and houses left them very well off in the post-war years).

You can make more money with real estate than you can with other investments. If you invest, say, $10,000 in the stock market, you may double your money (and if you double your money, count yourself extremely lucky). Ten thousand put into a $100,000 house will make you $100,000 if the value of the house doubles! On top of this, you can use money other than your own to make these profits. Other forms of investments require you to pay the full price of the goods you are buying. Real estate investments only require that you pay five percent to twenty percent of the price of the property—and you can avoid paying even that much, with the right techniques.

So, real estate is an investment in an absolute necessity, you can possess it for a fraction of its total cost, it is almost guaranteed to go up in value (if maintained well), and you do not have to use your own money to get it! In real estate, you can borrow the money you need to invest and later have your buyers or renters pay back those loans! Does this sound too much like a fairy tale? It's not. You can truly count on real estate investments.

Men have been investing in real estate for years. It is time we women realized why, and began making the same moves men have so that we, too, can forge profitable careers and have more freedom in our work. Real estate can be the ultimate career for a woman, and the best part is, you probably already have all the skills you need!

Real estate has certainly proved profitable for at least three women. In 1981, we—Jane Fowler, Lynda Frank, and Carol Wilson—were schoolteachers in our hometown of Kansas City. One of us had just gone through a divorce and was struggling to raise two boys by herself on a teacher's salary. Needless to say, she did not have much more than a dime (if that!) of extra income at the end of the month. The other two were not in the same financial straits but were looking for a tax break, a more promising retirement, and possibly a more stimulating career.

About this time, Jane read in the newspaper that a real estate seminar was coming to town. The ad said that the initial meeting was free and listed several exciting topics which would be explained. Jane decided to attend the free portion to see what she could learn, and her husband decided to go with her.

She called her friend, Lynda, and asked her to go along and Lynda agreed. The day of the seminar, as they were preparing to leave, the phone rang. It was Carol, a friend of Jane's since college, and Carol asked what Jane was doing. Jane explained where she was going, and Carol said she would like to come along. She had wanted to buy a rental house for twenty years but didn't know how to begin.

We'll let Jane tell you how it happened: "That evening the three of us, and my husband Jim, listened as new ideas were presented which sounded unbelievable. The speaker talked for two hours, and then tried to get us to sign up for a weekend course. It was very appealing, but also very expensive. Jim, however, encouraged us to sign up. He kept saying, 'You three can do it.'

"With shaky hands we took out our charge cards and signed up for what has proven to be the most exciting weekend and the springboard to all the opportunities I had hoped for, and even more. It was the most exciting course I had ever attended, and believe me, teachers have attended a few courses! I was so excited that I began to study everything I could get my hands on to learn all I could about investing.

"At school, I couldn't wait for my students to go to recess so I could race to the teacher's lounge to devour the ads. I listened to tapes as I drove around town in my car-pool duties. I cooked with the telephone in one hand as I was learning to screen the ads. I made phone call after phone call during my free time.

"Neither Lynda, Carol, nor I had had any prior experience, but we did have enthusiasm, as you will, too, after you are aware of the unlimited possibilities and rewards of this business."

Before we knew it, that school year had ended and we had discovered the perfect investment properties. We formed a legal partnership and each borrowed $4,000 from the bank (we have never put any more than that amount of our own money into our investments). This took care of our down payment and the renovation of the properties.

We were nervous, but we did it. We bought three properties (two five-plexes and one four-plex—we don't recommend this for everybody's first buy, but it worked for us) and worked on them all summer. When we had them dressed up and polished, we rented them out and got a positive cash flow going. This investment continues to bring in money for us, and the properties are building equity with each month that passes. They also allowed us to pay less to Uncle Sam that year.

Did we quit after that smashing success? Nope! Are we still excited about the idea? You bet! We are still buying, renting, and selling properties—we have done so well that we were able to give up our teaching jobs and take on real estate full time. We are now making more money and at the same time saving for our retirement. *And* using our brains most productively.

Real estate investing is a great career for us, and we intend to prove this to other women who have either not considered it an option or have decided that only men can succeed in it. (Real estate is a great career not only for men, but for women too.) We feel that women are naturals in the field. Why? Because women are so involved in buying a house that they understand what it takes to make a house marketable. Ask any real estate agent who has the final say in whether a couple buys or rents a house and he will give the same answer: the woman.

A woman, when shopping for a place to live for just herself or her family, will almost always be more discerning than a man is. Women usually spend more time in the home and value the way it looks more than the typical man. Thus, a woman investor can clean and/or decorate a property so that another woman would like it, leaving that home likely to be sold or rented more quickly. Women know what women want, and women make the final decisions in buying or renting a home—it is as simple as that. Women should therefore be more involved in the buying, selling, and renting process.

In addition, there are other skills that most women have developed through running a home. Women are now price conscious, since they do most of the shopping. Any wife and mother will admit that she has had to develop a great many organizational skills, skills that she uses daily. Women who direct households must know how to plan, budget, and solve problems—all necessary skills in real estate. The techniques that you already use to keep your children from killing each other and your home from falling apart will be indispensable to you in this new career.

There are other reasons a woman should be involved in real estate investments. With real estate investing, you can prove and fulfill yourself in an important role—people need housing and you are giving it to them. You can free yourself from the restrictions of a regular eight to five job, leaving more time to spend with your family or friends. You can open up your horizons by being financially independent, even wealthy. The amount of money to be made in real estate, unlike most other jobs, is not a fixed amount that goes up only when your employer is feeling generous; your pay is contingent upon you and how much energy you put into your new venture. If you work, you'll be reimbursed well in the form of lots of money. Imagine possessing a credit card with no overdue bills arriving on it, no outrageous interest to be paid because you can pay those bills the day they arrive and not when your other bills leave room to take care of them. Just think: Christmas would no longer be a problem. If you are happy with your present job, you can use real estate as a sideline, giving yourself extra money and tax savings. In this field your success is up to you and no one else.

Think of what this means. With real estate as your career, when you want to take a vacation, there will be no one to ask except yourself. If you want to take a day off, you will have that option. If you are a mother, you can stay home with a sick child, instead of having to take him to a baby-sitter who hates sick children. You can have lunch with your friends more often, or accompany your husband on business trips.

A career in real estate offers a woman more freedom than you probably ever thought possible. You say that the grocery store cashier is too busy at 5:30? You want to get your hair cut during the day instead of at night? You won't mind the time that you take off when you are your own boss! You like to read the paper after your children are on their way to school? Go right ahead! You feel your children would do better in school if you were at home at the end of the day? So true! You would have time to make those beds if you didn't leave for work until nine. Have lunch with your mom today. . . it's her birthday. Take the dog to get dipped for those fleas before the house is totally infested! But best of all, when the school calls to say that your child has a fever, you can go pick him up. The list can go on forever. This is the ultimate career for a woman. And you need so little to get started.

America is the land of opportunity. However, when many women hear this, they unconsciously make the sentence apply only to men. It is time to change that. America is the land of opportunity for both men and women, and it is time we women used this opportunity, along with our talents, to catch up with the men in this country who have done so well financially.

What talents, you say? Many women take their talents so much for granted that they do not even recognize they have them. But consider a woman's role in our society: How many men could perform all the tasks that a woman does and still smile? Whether she is single or married, a mother or childless, working or not, there are hundreds of skills that a woman possesses that she does not even recognize. We have already said that a woman running a home has many talents. She is a *time manager;* somehow she has learned to do ten things at once. She shops, she cooks, she cleans, she organizes, she budgets, she schedules, she chauffeurs, she is a recreational planner, she handles crisis management, she becomes a building-and-grounds maintenance engineer, a social affairs director, and a guidance counselor.

Consider some of the talents that you might possess but never stop to think about. As a woman, you are probably in charge of *purchasing* to assure an adequate supply of needed products. Your goal is to acquire these products within a limited, budgeted amount of available funds. *Inventory control* becomes one of your assets. Poor inventory control becomes a great time waster and leads to an inefficiently run household.

As a woman, you may be totally in charge of *transportation* within your household. You must assure maximum utilization of a limited motor pool, often meeting conflicting schedules which necessitate arrangements for additional vehicles.

You may also have assumed the role of *guidance counselor* for many years without even noticing, or giving yourself any credit for the knowledge and expertise that you have gained through experience.

Women simply do not realize how valuable they are. Consider what a secretary does for a company. Where would American business be without secretaries to keep everything organized and on time? What man could have ten projects thrown at him at once and not collapse or revolt? Women handle this sort of demand every day. By our nature and upbringing, women are skilled in handling crises. Consider a man's abilities (or inabilities) when shopping. How many men do you know who have the patience to shop for a good buy?

A man's impulse is to grab the first object suitable for his needs, buy it, and leave the store. It is his nature.

Real estate investing requires the talents that most women have developed. It is necessary for a person to handle several tasks at one time—it also requires organizational skills: negotiating, budgeting, time management, bookkeeping, even decorating. Smart investors need to know how to shop for properties. Once the investment properties are bought, they must be made ready for rent or sale. How many men can efficiently clean, fix up, and decorate a house with a minimum of time and money? A man is very likely to call in a woman to help him with this task.

Do you begin to see what we so excitedly recognized a few years ago? Women are naturals in the real estate investment field. But don't take our word for it alone. See the list below of some of the different situations a woman can find herself in today, and note how well a career in real estate investing would suit all of them.

A married, working mother: You are putting in forty hours a week. Your children are in a child-care center or a public school. Your rigid schedule makes it impossible to attend your daughter's school play or go on business trips when your husband invites you. Out of financial necessity, you must work. Real estate investing, worked even part time, can easily replace that $10,000 to $20,000 a year that you make, and can give you more freedom. You could be free for spontaneous events with your family and would never again have to send a sick child to school because you couldn't stay home with him. Your schedule could become yours, and if a crisis came up, you could simply call your realtor and cancel your plans to shop for houses at 1:30. You could go another time.

Divorced, mother or childless: Get revenge on your husband! Show him the true creative and intellectual genius that is no longer a part of his life. Make more money than he does. If you have overcome the need for revenge against your ex, then just console yourself with the prospect of living better. If you have children, how can you provide for their educations? Where can you get the money for those dancing lessons your daughter needs? Or glasses or braces? When one of us was in this situation, her accountant advised her to go into real estate, saying, "You don't have anywhere to go but up!" You are probably in the same circumstance. It is very difficult to try to raise children on your own; it leaves you full of fears that you will not be able to care for your children financially.

Many single-parent homes headed by women are living under the poverty level. Brace yourself and ask the question: Am I broke most of the time? Can I count on child support? Have I enough extra income to even take the kids on a vacation once every five years? You can change your situation, and without even waiting for that winning lottery ticket.

Single, working in any position that pays less than $14,000 a year: You are intelligent, creative, and have few ways to express this. You do not receive much pay now, but you have hopes of working your way up the ladder. But at what level will you find yourself in a dead end? Will you finish your climb as a supervisor who makes $24,000 a year? You could make that much annually on the side through real estate investing.

Married, working, no children: You have your own career, whether you want it or not. If you like what you are doing, work real estate on the side to provide for an extended trip to Europe or South America. If you don't like what you're doing but you must work, leave that job and do something more stimulating without a boss or begin investing on the side until you can.

Widowed: An emotionally and financially trying position. This is a difficult period in your life, especially if it just happened. Investing will give you back that temporarily lost sense of purpose, force you to use your mental and creative powers and *make you money.* You probably need the latter most acutely now, or did that ample (?) insurance policy leave you set for life? We're not making light of your situation; we only wish you to face your future, especially if you have young children.

Married, with or without children, not working: Your husband makes enough money so you do not have to work. You are at home alone, or with the kids. Are you tired of soap operas, cleaning house, and crafts? Are you dying to talk to another adult and to feel a sense of purpose? Well, we promise you that home owners, real estate agents, and bankers are all over eighteen. We are also certain that you would feel a sense of achievement in buying and selling houses. Say good-bye to boredom and hello to extra dollars. Spend as little or as much time as you choose. You can catch up on those soaps every few weeks anyway!

Just out of high school and don't want to go to college, or, worse, you don't have the money to go to college: In real estate, you don't need a degree! You could decide to work as a secretary or a clerk, but where will that leave you in six years? Will you be well off? Will you have an education? You could go to night school and receive a degree in eight or nine years, or you could start reading about real estate now and have a nice career or make enough to go to school. Try to make your decision now, at seventeen or eighteen, as to what you intend to do with the rest of your life (it's not easy, we know, but try). Do you want to slave until you retire? Or slave until you possibly marry and then slave even more while raising children? Real estate offers you far more options. The three of us realize that if we had started learning at that age, there is no telling what we could be worth!

In college or just out of college: Learn about real estate to complement your other studies. Buy your first home! If you are still attending college, live in your property and rent out the rest. You will be building equity, and with the rent payments you collect, you lower (if not eliminate) your housing costs. If you have just graduated, perhaps you are having a tough time finding a job. Use your spare time to gain knowledge of real estate investing. Keep in mind that Mom and Dad, more often than not, cut off funds to their offspring once the mortarboards have been worn. You are going to need an income. And real estate investing certainly beats waitressing.

An older woman ready to join the work force, either for the first time or after a long period of time: You're worried; you feel you do not have adequate skills to be working, but you are bored. Maybe you need to work; maybe you feel you have not set aside enough for your retirement. Real estate investments are the perfect solution to your problem. You have the skills you need—you proved that by running a home successfully. You can handle the challenge that investments will give you. You will be making money for a satisfactory retirement, and you will no longer be bored. Even if you dropped out of school in eighth grade! Who cares—no resume required here! Prove to yourself that you are smart after all!

Married to a professional and no need for extra income because you pay enough to Uncle Sam already: You could get into real estate investing and provide your husband with a way to stop paying so much in taxes. Because housing is so vital, anyone who provides it gets a major tax break. And real estate investing is more exciting than tennis, bridge, or tea with the neighbors. Plus there's a bonus: you could end up making more than your lawyer- or doctor-husband with your investments, and have something to discuss at dinner besides politics!

A woman professional: You, too, are probably paying out quite a bit of money come April 15. Buy a few homes and use that money on a vacation home in the mountains, or in the Caribbean.

A woman whose husband is already in real estate investing: We are talking here to you ladies whose men have bought the books on investment and are excited about it. Don't resent this newfound interest of his—listen to what he is saying at the dinner table and catch those figures. The two of you will make a great team!

A woman who would like to start her own business but lacks capital: You've had a life-long ambition to open your own business. Real estate investments might make this dream a reality. And that income will continue coming in, even if (perish the thought, but it does happen in four out of five cases) your dream venture sputters out. The scent of bankruptcy will stay on one's records like the smell of rotting fish in the refrigerator; a steady income outside of your dream-come-true can help avoid that stench.

A mother concerned for her child's future: In this case, forget the extra income, the tax breaks, and luxuries that real estate investing can provide—wouldn't you just like to provide your child with a nice present once he (or she) is ready to leave your care? What will that sixty dollar watch do for him after he has been on his own for five years? Instead, consider buying him a real gift now, in the form of a house. You can rent it out until he is ready to take it over (giving *yourself* a tax break and some extra income), and then give it to him when he is ready for it. He could then live in it himself or continue renting it. He could borrow against it to start his own business. He could sell it and leave the country to explore the world. Or, let it be the monthly paycheck that allows him to go to school. You think they're too young to warrant any concern with college yet? Have you even a guess as to how much it will cost by the year 2000 to put a person through college?

Pregnant: Are you not working those last few months? Consider dedicating a few days a week to looking for a good investment property. Buying a couple of homes now could allow your baby to live in a nicer home, grow up in a better neighborhood, attend nicer schools, give him fun and educational toys (computers for kids are expensive) or send him to camp. (However much you love the child that rests in your womb just now, there may be a time, ten years or so down the line, when you both might want a vacation from one another.) Being a mother is so much more enjoyable when you have more cash in the bank.

During maternity leave, you can learn more about investing. Your boss is expecting you back when? You get tears in your eyes just thinking about it! A career in investment allows a woman the freedom to slow down to have a baby. She can forget the boss anxiously awaiting her return in six weeks. A career where you can breast-feed a baby? Too good to be true.

Unemployed: What have you got to lose? If you are receiving an unemployment check right now, don't stop, but try studying real estate investments for three months. Look for a good buy and get started with your own career while the U.S. government is helping you. You will soon be secure in a field where no boss can fire you and no company will fold and leave you without an income. Maybe you could move in with your parents or a friend until you get going. But do get going. Unemployment is hard on one's self-esteem.

On welfare: This, too, is hard on self-esteem. We recognize that it is a very difficult situation to break out of, but that does not mean that it cannot be done. Read every book you can find at the library on real estate investments. Study the ads in the paper. Begin building your credit rating (we will help you with this) and start shopping for a house. You deserve a better life than you have, and you can have it with self-discipline and some self-teaching. Far more difficult situations than yours have been overcome in the history of humankind—you can do it if you've the will to do it.

Not married, but in love or engaged: This situation can go along with many of the above. There are lots of nice restaurants and vacation spots you and your boyfriend could visit with some added income. You could plan for a nice honeymoon, if you're planning to get married. You could pay for a lovely wedding. A large bank account makes for a healthier marriage—it would be nice if all a couple needed was love, but this world requires money, unfortunately. And financial problems wreak havoc with marriages.

Married and wishing you weren't: Your husband goes off to work every day after a quick peck on the cheek. Maybe you work, maybe you don't, but it's the same, same, same every dull, dull, dull day. You want out, but you're scared to make a move. What will you live on? Who will support you? You can support yourself with a few smart investments, and you can leave behind that need to share your husband's income along with your husband. We do not condone getting into real estate to leave your husband, but we are aware that many marriages are not as blissful as our own, and with your own source of income, the wrong marriage can become the right divorce. Whatever the reason for your unhappiness with your spouse, real estate can give you something more to think about. There is an escape!

We have given you many situations. If we missed yours, we apologize, but we are confident that some real estate investments could change your life for the better if you are presently unhappy with your situation.

A career in real estate investing will allow you to wear many different costumes. How could you possibly become bored with a career in which one day you wear a suit to see your banker and the next you wear your overalls to wallpaper the room? No two days are alike, and you get paid well for your efforts. In real estate investing, you are a person who solves problems—a real troubleshooter. You are solving a major problem for people by finding them places to live or taking a home off their hands that is perhaps eating up their precious income. And no other investment allows you to borrow the money to make that investment, or allows other people to make the payments on that borrowed money for you.

Another reason for women to get into real estate investing is one of the main reasons we got into it: self-esteem. To take on a venture and succeed at it financially heightened our self-esteem greatly. We three feel we are doing something worthwhile and exciting—we feel that we are helping society. We know we're good landlords (there are many who are not), and that people who buy the homes we have renovated are happy with their choices. In teaching, we were helping the children we taught, yes, but not one of us could see doing that for thirty-five more years and then retiring. We feel that the time we gave to educating young people was time well spent, but, quite frankly, it was becoming boring. Not to mention a dead end financially, since considering the four hours of overtime every night, teaching is a poorly paid profession.

Also, teaching did not remain a challenge. Every day, every year, was basically the same as the last. Investing in rental housing, however, is a challenge. We feel that we are contributing something to our marriages and preparing for our eventual retirement, which gives us a wonderful feeling of accomplishment. We sleep well at night (even though we often wake up with great ideas for more investments!), and we are happy with ourselves, which we think, is a rarity; many women are not happy with themselves.

Why are most women not happy with themselves? The reasons are many, but almost all of them are involved with the society in which we live and what it has taught us. Although our society is changing, women, who are actually a majority of the population, are often treated as a *minority*. The socioeconomic factors for this are endless, and established on hundreds of years of precedent, but one of the major reasons that women are in this position is because of a lack of money. Money. Property. Barter power. Most of the money and property in the world is owned by men. And money is power. Like it or not, that's the way it is.

Owning property is like having money in the bank. Both men and women benefit from more equal (but not necessarily the same) roles in society. Real estate investing is a step in that direction for all women: property owners have more influence in, and gain more respect from, society. We want to see more women become property owners because this leads to a more balanced society, happier relationships, and better marriages. And we think all women and men deserve this.

We hope we have convinced you that any woman is qualified for real estate investing and to make a go of it. You are not too old. You are not too weak. You are not too unskilled, and you are not too uneducated. Even a woman in a wheelchair can get into real estate investing and make it work for her. As a matter of fact, we saw a woman in a wheelchair at one of the seminars we went to. She had two younger people with her who could have been her partners. She is truly a courageous woman trying to better her situation. A disabled woman could do the phone work, search the ads, do the bookkeeping. You see, there is a way for everyone to get into this field. Those of you who feel that you cannot do the strenuous work of fixing up and decorating simply because you are female, can take it from us: you can do it. We have found that although one of us may not be able to do a task by herself, the three of us together can. So can you.

There is no reason to lack confidence in yourself—the world is not totally a man's domain. As a woman, you have the confidence and ability to succeed at any task. All you need to begin investing in homes are the following things: 1) an ambitious nature, (2) a need for self-fulfillment, (3) mathematical ability (or a calculator), (4) good judgment, and (5) self-discipline. No college education is necessary. Even a high school diploma is not required (we do, however, recommend that teenagers remain in school).

All you need is time to read and learn about real estate investing. You have to adjust to some new terms. Do not allow legal talk or indecipherable contracts to frighten you. It is all conquerable. And you'll be most adequately reimbursed for your hours devoted to your investments. Investments in rental housing are the means to a better life-style and a more secure future. We did it, and so can you.

CHAPTER TWO

Before
You Begin...

DOES WHAT YOU HAVE READ so far sound too good to be true? That was our first reaction when we attended that first seminar. Rest assured, real estate investing is not too good to be true. It has worked for us during a time when many were saying "The glory days of real estate ended with the seventies."

Before you go rushing out to buy the first low-priced fixer-upper you see, perhaps you should sit down and consider some important questions. By doing this now, you can avoid entering into a financial situation you might not wish to be in later. At this point, you need to assess who you are and what your own needs are. What do you want from your investments? You also need to know what to expect before you step into the challenging but rewarding field of real estate.

Ask yourself some questions. Why does real estate investing sound so good to you? What have you read so far in this book that has you interested? This is important because there are many different types of investing for you to get involved in. You could invest in land, apartment buildings, duplexes, condominiums, office buildings, or shopping centers, as well as single-family homes. Some of these are obviously very expensive and involve more complicated financing and knowledge of investing techniques. Assuming this is the first book you've read on real estate investments, complicated deals are likely to be beyond your purchasing ability just now. Thus, we shall talk about more simple forms of investing: single-family homes, duplexes, condominiums, and small apartment houses. Consider this a course in beginning real estate investing.

It is important that you realize there are different ways to get money back from your investments. With some investments you will be paid off quickly, in others, the benefits come over a long period of time. The former could be better if you need cash in a hurry; the latter is better if you want a sustained income or are planning on using investments as a way to provide for your retirement. You need to ascertain exactly what you need before you can begin moving in the direction that is best for you.

There are many different types of investments in real estate. Probably the most popular is investments in single-family homes. These seem to be the easiest to sell as well as quite easy to rent. This does not mean they're always the best place to put your money (remember that our first purchase was three multi-unit dwellings), it simply means they are the most common real estate investment. Many investors feel that houses are the safest type of property to buy because most people are looking for single-family homes instead of bigger and more expensive multi-family units. We, however, have not lost anything by our decision, and in fact are very happy with those first properties that we bought four years ago.

It depends on your needs. We own those three properties and they are building equity for us each day. They're a marvelous tax shelter, and at the same time, our tenants are paying for them in the form of rent payments. We have money left over from those rent payments each month, after all our monthly bills are paid on those properties—a positive cash flow. This is exactly what we wanted. A negative cash flow—one in which we paid out more than we took in on a certain property—would not do at all. No equity that is being built is worth financial loss. Many of you probably want a positive monthly cash flow situation, instead of large amounts of money all at once, just as we did. We will talk more about this when we discuss purchasing your first house. Right now, what you need to do is assess what you want from your investments. Once you decide what you want from your investing career, you can begin reading the books and materials related to your goals.

Perhaps what you're looking for is a healthy retirement: You would like to reap most of the rewards for your hard work when you're older. Again, what you want is a positive cash flow. If you are holding on to your present job and just thinking of this as a way to a secure future, you are probably not so concerned with making a large profit on your properties each month after your payments have been made because you have your paycheck to live on. Your best bet, then, is to find and buy a few properties now and rent them out, thereby leaving someone else to make your payments for you, and watch your equity grow as you grow older. Your retirement is set. By the time you reach sixty-five, you will have quite a bit of equity built up in your properties (the amount of this equity, of course, depends on your age when you bought your homes) and you can either sell them and live on that money, continue renting them out, or refinance them in order for the government to allow you a tax-free income. The more houses you buy now, the bigger your retirement fund.

Also ask yourself whether you want to approach this as a full-time or a part-time endeavor. Are you happy in your present job? Then real estate will be a supplement to your present income and not your primary source of income. This is an important difference. If real estate will be your primary source of income, you are going to have more time to devote to it (it is, after all, your job—you spend 40 hours a week at any other job, and so it is with this one, though in this job you set your hours). If you have more time to spend with it, you have more time to search out those great buys. And, if this is your job—your primary source of income—you need a healthy enough cash flow that you can live on it. This obviously means you must buy more properties than the person who wants simply to retire comfortably or have a supplemental income. We worked our two careers—teaching and real estate investing—concurrently for two years before we felt secure enough to leave the classroom and become full-time investors. We now put in more hours of work time than we did teaching, but our time is more flexible and we consider it pleasurable. This is a major consideration: Do you want to eventually make investing your only career? If so, you need to approach it more seriously and buy more homes than the part-time investor.

Maybe you want to invest in real estate as a tax shelter. You or your husband make plenty of money to live on and you would like to give less of this hard-earned cash to the government. Rental housing is a solution to your problem. Buying houses and quickly selling them for a profit without renting them will not help you with your tax problem. On the contrary, it makes Uncle Sam all the more interested in you. Always keep in mind that the IRS has a legal right to a part of your income—if you take in large sums of cash by buying and selling homes for a profit, you must report it. That will put you into a higher tax bracket than you are in already, and you'll be paying out even more in taxes. This is not exactly what you hope to get out of investing, is it?

However, there is a way to use both renting and selling techniques in your investments. Many investors who have turned real estate buys into a very lucrative profession use both a quick sale—thus quick cash—and rentals; this way they make big money and yet pay minimal taxes. You, too, could do this one day, but it takes time and hard work. If you've sufficient funds, a great job, and no need to be rich, then use your investments as a tax break only. You need to look for properties that can easily be made into rentals, thereby giving you the write-off you seek.

We spoke of quick profits in that last paragraph—did that catch your eye? Many people need quick profits. Perhaps you've a debt to pay off, or maybe you have a business venture in mind that requires capital. Or perhaps the idea of having a large amount in your bank account simply appeals to you. Whatever your reason, you would like to have a quick profit and you think that real estate can provide you with it. As we have said, it can, but we would like to define the word *quick*. A quick profit in real estate does not always mean that you can go out today, find the perfect house, buy it, and have it sold—with cash in hand—by next Monday. Closings are very vital aspects of real estate transactions, and they take a notoriously long time to transpire. You can usually count on a six-week delay between the time your offer on a property is accepted and the time the closing actually takes place. After you own the house, you must do any rehabilitating that needs to be done. Once that is completed, you need to put that property on the market and wait for it to sell. How quickly it sells depends upon how badly you want your quick profit—you are now in the position of being a "don't wanter," the type of buyer that you looked for in order to purchase your home in the first place (we'll explain this later). Add on another six weeks before the closing of your sale takes place, and you're getting an idea of what quick means in this field. Your house will sell, and you will make a profit, but it will take time. Count on at least three months before your first quick profit, and make your plans for the use of your money accordingly.

Another item to think about is whether you plan on doing the rehabilitation of your homes yourself. At first we did most of our own cleaning and redecorating, but now that we are more successful and confident with our investments, we don't do as much. We did it before because we were concerned that we would make less profit by paying someone else to do it than if we did it ourselves. This is a good point. You can save quite a bit of money by doing your own rehabs. But we also found, after we became more experienced, that by letting others do this work for us we can make even more money by using the time we spent cleaning carpets to buy more homes that add to our cash flow. The cost of having such chores done for us is more than compensated by these new profits. When we first started, however, we simply did not have the money to have anyone do this work for us. We had to do the cleaning and redecorating if it was going to be done at all. During this period, we also learned what it costs to renovate a property, enabling us to make better judgments now. You might be in this same position. Whatever your decision on this, keep in mind that to hire work done on a house is to cut out of your profits.

A most important aspect to consider is just how much cash you are willing or able to put into your investment. Perhaps you have quite a sum to invest—this allows you to make a healthy down payment and you have a wider market to work within. Suppose, however, that you haven't any money to make a down payment. In this case, your market is narrowed (but by no means eliminated!). With no money down, you must look for some form of special financing. Such arrangements are to be found, but you have to know what you are looking for and how to ask for it. It is possible. Remember—all of our properties were bought with *none* of our own money.

Consider all the aspects we have discussed previously. You will not know where you're going unless you know what your personal cash requirements are. If you don't have a "game plan" you can make mistakes. And that's what we're trying to help you avoid, by asking you to define your needs.

Once you have decided what your financial needs are, you can move on to setting up some specific goals to be realized from your real estate investments.

Ask yourself about goals. What goals have you presently set for yourself? What are your lifetime goals? What do you want to accomplish in the next year, five years, etc.? If you knew you would die six months from today, how would you live until then? Do you have any goals at all right now?

The three of us are great believers in goals. We feel that once you have a defined objective in mind and *on paper,* you tend to move more directly toward it, instead of wandering about. Scattered, unorganized ideas will get you nowhere. We have goals we've written down and frequently refer back to, asking: What goals have we attained? Which ones are we still working on? We once set a goal of owning over one million dollars worth of property by October 1983. We reached that goal at a closing on September 29 of that year. Another goal was to "zero out" on our income tax returns—we achieved that the second year of investing. Without a concrete idea of what we were working toward, we probably would not have accomplished those goals.

All of the books you read on successful living stress that you must *write down* your goals. And don't just write them down and put them where you can forget them—put them in a place where you are constantly reminded of them. Don't feel embarrassed or silly about it—people who have goals are winners! Do you think champion athletes just casually go out to train without a specific goal in mind? Of course not. They are participating in a training program to win, and having goals is a major part of that program, as is their attitude. So write down your goals, whatever they pertain to. It will make your life better. We think you should write down a set of specific goals for your investing plans and hopes too. It will be your road map of where to go and when to do what.

In setting up your goals for your investing career, give yourself a time frame. Make a deadline for yourself: I will have such and such done by such and such date. In making this deadline, be fair to yourself. To write: I will be a millionaire by this time next year, is *not* being fair to yourself. It is unrealistic and, if such a goal is not attained, it leaves you discouraged and unwilling to try anything more. To say that you'll be a millionaire in five years, however, *is* reasonable.

When making deadlines for yourself, anticipate and plan for problems that might arise. Mentally check your progress frequently and, if necessary, reset your goals, but don't use this as an excuse to keep procrastinating—there is a difference between resetting your goals and avoiding the work necessary to realize them. Write down who is involved in your goals. Describe where you will accomplish those goals; for example, in what neighborhood will most of your properties be. Write out why you are seeking those goals, and how you will overcome any problems you confront.

Now that you have done this, refine your goals by picking out the three that are most important. Use these goals to write a detailed statement of personal goals. From here, list the activities you think will be involved in accomplishing each goal. Gather as much information as you possibly can through study, meetings, and conversation. Brainstorm your alternative courses of action and identify the problems you think might come up. Select the most appropriate actions and begin your plan of action by setting your *start date*. Follow your action plan as closely as possible.

To set up a specific timetable like this leaves you little room to feel that you don't know what to do any single day to push yourself toward achieving your investment goals.

Remember to constantly evaluate your progress toward those goals. We three do this by a three-way telephone call (it isn't very expensive and it's certainly worth it) at 8:30 every morning after our children are off to school. We discuss what we accomplished for our partnership the day before and what we plan to accomplish during the day. And we always look at our progress with a positive attitude. If you haven't got a partner yet, or do not intend to have one, talk over your goals with a close friend. Talk helps so much—it's what we women are good at, isn't it? Everyone needs a support system, whether it is personal or professional, and that is what talking provides.

Remember to ask these questions: What did I do today? What did it accomplish? What did I plan to do today? Are the answers to these questions the same? If not, what will you do about it tomorrow and why *didn't* you do it today? Do not baby yourself. We women are tough and we can take asking tough questions of ourselves.

Time Management

Once you have your goals set, you will probably find yourself needing to rearrange the use of your time. You will soon learn that time is the most valuable thing you possess. There is a reason employers are so picky about time not being wasted at work: time is money. Successful people are careful with their time and refuse to waste it.

There are several things you can do to help you save your precious time. First of all, list what you think are time wasters. Once you have identified these, try to eliminate them. How important is it that you watch that night-time soap opera? Could you possibly give up some of the time you spend talking to your neighbors about your lawn? If you consider your day, you will find that many hours are spent in non-productive tasks. They are enjoyable, but they are not getting you anywhere.

Identify some key concepts of good time management. You have to run the car pool for your kids' soccer game? Use that time wisely. As you drive, listen to some investment or motivational tapes in your car (your kids may not be wild about them, but they aren't putting bread on the table, either). Read a book on different methods to finance your investments or go over the ads while you wait for them. Perhaps you could draw up your list for tasks to be done tomorrow. Whatever you do, just don't allow that time to be wasted.

We evaluate the time we spend in a particular area or task and then, if we find it necessary, decide what needs to be done to change or eliminate the task. We also try to expect the unexpected and plan for it. Every hour we spend in constructive planning saves us three or four hours in execution. Thus, we have better and faster results.

We recommend that you use long-range and daily planning to achieve the most effective use of your time. Allow some flexibility in your scheduling; this enables you to adjust to outside forces beyond your control. We try to schedule enough time to accomplish our tasks, but we have a habit of usually making our deadlines too close, thus giving ourselves more stress. But we feel that the faster we complete any given project, especially a house rehabilitation, the faster it will make us money.

Set priorities for yourself through careful planning—make up an ordered sequence based on what your priorities are. Such priorities and time management give you self-discipline, something you really must have when working for yourself. You will also find that you will be less likely to procrastinate or be indecisive. Remember, when you are investing in homes, there is no one to tell you what to do or when to do it. You have left your boss behind—you are responsible for your own time and actions without him. Now you've no one to blame but yourself if a task doesn't get done.

Always have an alternative plan—this will allow you to select the most effective course of action. And make sure you consolidate similar tasks. For instance, if you are going to the courthouse to look up a title on a house you're interested in, check on a few other properties that you had planned to look up next week. You've saved yourself a trip (and gas, an important factor in these energy-conserving days). Group your tasks to be completed into divisions of your work day. This economizes your time and effort and allows you to concentrate on the critical events of the day. And always, try to *do the right job right!* Your efforts are wasted if you do the wrong tasks at the wrong time. And don't spend as much time on tasks that are low on your priority list as you do on those that are on the top. Those items at the top are there for a reason.

Here's a tip: Each of us has a list of goals written down which we keep where we can see it daily—in the kitchen and on the bathroom mirror. You can't accomplish what you can't remember.

Once you get going with investing, you will find that you have many tasks to do and think about. But don't be overwhelmed by them. Remember that some problems will go away by themselves. Also, do not treat every problem as a crisis. Nothing is forever—only living and dying. Life is difficult when fears are plaguing you. We've enough built-in fears—don't add to them. This will cause anxiety, wrong judgments, and incorrect decisions, all of which are a waste of time. And we are trying to eliminate the time wasters so that we can be more productive.

Self-image and attitude are important too. Setting up goals will not do much for you if you lack self-esteem. Take this assessment of yourself a step further: Do you like yourself? Do you have much confidence in your abilities? Do you believe in yourself, or are you quick to say "that's impossible"? Would you say that you are a positive or a negative person? If you have a less than healthy view of yourself and a negative attitude, you are not alone in your lack of self-confidence, nor are you a hopeless case. You simply need to approach yourself and the world differently.

You need to change your self-image; you need to learn to like that person you see in the mirror. You also need to learn to expect the best instead of gloomily expecting failure. You must believe in yourself and not approach new ideas and unfamiliar tasks with a negative attitude. You can do anything you set your mind to. Try to catch yourself when you begin to cut yourself down, either verbally or mentally. Women are great ones for this. They are forever telling themselves "I am too fat," " . . . too ugly," " . . . too dumb," etc. What you are is . . . too negative.

To succeed in real estate investing, it is very important that you develop a healthy sense of self-esteem and a positive attitude. We will stress the need for a positive attitude frequently throughout the book, but you may want to read a couple of books devoted to helping you build confidence and self-esteem. Such books will help you in every facet of your life, not just in your investing career. Go to the library and see what you can find that can teach you to enjoy seeing your face each morning in the mirror.

Be positive in every situation. It makes your day go better and it leaves other people feeling happier—they also tend to imitate your optimistic nature. Avoid going into a situation and looking for the negative aspects of it. Instead, concentrate on the positive. There are positive aspects everywhere you go, no matter what type of world the evening news portrays. A positive attitude is especially important in real estate investing. A blue mood can destroy a deal. You need to approach your work positively, expecting everything to work out. You need to use your creativity to eliminate any negative aspects—you should never concentrate on them.

In our partnership, Carol is the positive "I can do anything" personality. All three of us are optimistic people, but her never-say-die manner especially rubs off on us so we all maintain a good attitude about our present deals and possible buys. Such an attitude is essential. If you expect good and do good, it comes rolling in to you on a conveyor belt. By the same token, if you expect the opposite, troubles will plague you.

So like yourself! Expect the best! And have confidence in what you are doing! It will make your day and your new career roll along so much more smoothly.

Now let's deal with some fears that might be on your mind. The one question we get asked most often by investors-to-be is whether we aren't afraid of our financial situation. People want to know if our debts (in the form of loans we've taken out to buy our properties) frighten us. Well, they don't, for two reasons. First, our debts are far exceeded by what others—our tenants and those whom we have sold houses to via owner financing—owe us. If anybody does not pay their bills, we have the right to take action in order to get that money, or to remove them from our property and find someone else who will pay their bills. (We should mention here that this seldom happens—we screen our tenants and buyers carefully.) And second, each of us has only put a $4,000 initial investment into this business. Though $4,000 is not a small sum of money, it is hardly a fortune. If we lost it all due to some nationwide economic problems or by some hasty business deal (the latter is not likely) then we would each be out only that $4,000. And, as we have knowledge and capability, we could start again, and we would.

There are other fears that beginning investors feel. At first you may be nervous about each necessary step. Calling an owner with a house for sale could make you excessively fearful. But it must be faced, so get yourself prepared, write out the questions that you would like to ask, and dial the phone. You will find that making those phone calls really isn't so bad. The first time you meet an owner to look at his home you might find yourself a bit apprehensive, but after that initial meeting, you'll find that you can have fun. When you are ready to make that first offer and you know you will probably have to negotiate, you might be very afraid. But if you are prepared to listen to the seller's needs and keep an open mind about the alternatives available if the seller doesn't accept your offer, you haven't failed. There is no reason to let a deal that doesn't come off frighten you.

We were afraid at first, too, but fear is a hurdle you can get over by taking one small step at a time. Collecting house payments or rent payments, making sure that a house does not have hidden loans against it that you as a buyer might be liable for, are examples of fears that could keep you up at nights if you are a real estate investor. Some uneasy feelings are more vague: they are the thoughts you never quite finish. Those *what-ifs*. Other fears are downright ridiculous: What if there is a law in this county against blondes buying a house? Such fears are laughable in the daylight, but at night all kinds of odd thoughts can creep into your mind, and they can be very troubling if they aren't dealt with. That's the trick—to find out what fear is making you balk and then analyzing it.

Some fears are well-grounded. For instance, a house that is worth $55,000 but has a great deal of back taxes owed on it would certainly leave us wary. Get to know your subject—real estate investments—and these fears will become controllable. Knowledge is the key here, as well as in almost every aspect of your life. If you *know* what you are doing, you will be able to keep your fears in the right perspective. Look at your fears rationally and work around them. To be cautious is one thing; to be afraid is quite another.

As long as we're talking about obstacles, let's talk about a major one: the opinions of others. You might as well prepare yourself for it now, ladies. Believe it or not, many of the people that you know are self-appointed experts on real estate—they know everything you don't about the subject, especially the reasons for you not to touch investing with a ten-foot pole. Never mind that they have never bought a home or read a book about it in their lives—they know what they are saying . . . they think. Your friends, relatives, perhaps even members of your immediate family will be ready to tell you that your dream of making a successful go of it in real estate investing simply will not work. You will hear even more of this because you are a woman. They will eye you skeptically and shake their heads. "Oh, no," they'll say, " you can't do that. It worked for them, but it won't for you."

Many people don't like new ideas, even if those new ideas don't affect them in the least. But before you fall prey to their pessimism, ask yourself: "Why *shouldn't* it work for me?" Do three school teachers have more of an inside line into the real estate market than you do? Just what do you think we knew that you don't? You have as many capabilities as we do. And remember that we began and succeeded at a time when no one was supposed to do well in real estate: home values, the papers told us, were stagnant and going nowhere. Well, we proved that with determination and some serious bargain shopping, good buys can be found. There are homes out there that owners need to sell and there are buyers who need to buy. Find them and close your ears to those boo-birds.

Boo-birds will tell you everything is impossible. They are the ones who told Columbus the world was flat. They were the ones who told the Indians to go ahead and sell Manhattan Island—its value would never go up. Be polite, but don't listen to their negativity, even if the speaker is your best friend. Some people are just negative by nature: that is the way they communicate. Don't let them stop you!

As long as we're talking about others' opinions, let's discuss a very sensitive issue. This concerns a certain segment of society, our counterparts—men. Once you are in the business of investing, you will find that most men will accept you and be encouraging. Male investors are usually interested in our techniques and want to hear about our successes—they respect us and are curious to talk with us. And you'll find that most male home owners treat you basically as though you are a prospective buyer, which makes sense, since that is exactly what you are. The majority of male bankers will be cordial enough—they would like to lend you money: the bank makes money when they do. Most men will be friendly and business-minded. But be prepared, ladies: there are men out there who will feel personally threatened by the thought of a female real estate investor.

Let's face it: it takes all kinds to make a world. There have to be paranoid men with fragile egos or we would not know how lucky we are to be women. Such men are going to feel uncomfortable, ill at ease, and just plain fearful of you. They may show it by being resentful, or perhaps even insulting. We have found that the best way to deal with such insecurities is by either ignoring them, or by being cool but polite. We have found strength in numbers; the fact that we are three women instead of one leaves few men ready to insult us. You may want to remember this when you are considering a partner.

Women have been dealing with unfair attitudes from men in the business world for quite a while. It unfortunately is a part of the game. Until we can totally eliminate insecurity and ego problems (don't hold your breath) from the world, women will just have to put up with it, whatever careers we pursue.

There are other men out there who may try to take advantage of you, thinking that a woman can't know much about business. Do not tolerate this. Shop prices for any service you require. Know what the usual rate for title insurance is, shop for a lawyer with reasonable rates, etc. Those you hire to do work on your houses are men you especially want to watch. Some workmen are convinced that a woman does not know a good job when she sees one, so they feel it makes no difference what type of work they do. They also feel that a woman will pay double what a man would pay. Avoid this by calling around before hiring anyone to do anything for you. To put up with an occasional nasty male's comments is one thing; to let somebody take advantage of you is quite another. Again, knowledge is the key. Be prepared for such assaults on your integrity, and deal with them as the situation dictates.

Unfortunately, there are people—both men and women—who feel no qualms about trying to cheat you. We three former teachers had an especially difficult time accepting this. But such is the world. Get used to it and be aware when a con job is being pulled on you.

However, there is a bright note to being a female investor, certain benefits to be reaped from men's attitudes toward women anywhere you go. For instance, a female landlord will find that her male tenants will often do simple tasks like changing a washer on a drippy faucet, redoing a window screen, etc. They do not like to ask a woman to do it. So don't fume about those narrow-minded men out there. Concentrate instead on the majority of men—they are decent

44

and supportive. Finding a few bad apples doesn't mean you should get angry at the whole bushel. Besides, anger only inhibits your abilities and slows you down. It's just not worth it.

Let's continue talking about men, but this time let's talk about some nicer guys—our husbands. Our husbands have been extremely accepting and encouraging as we have moved into real estate investing. They help us whenever possible and are proud of our accomplishments, but they had some new factors to get used to in our lives. In regard to any men who might be important to you, keep in mind that your career is as new for them as it is for you, and they will have some adjustments to make. You will be quite busy, and some of the time that you normally spend with them will be spent apart, mainly evenings. They won't like this. All you can do is explain that it is part of your new work schedule. Try going out to lunch with your man as often as possible (without a boss, you'll be able to do things like this more often). At first, your husband may have a tough time when he answers the phone. No, the receiver has not grown any heavier; it's the voice on the other end that upsets him. It's deep, it's male, and it's asking for you! Never mind that it's just your realtor—why is he calling you? Men just have a hard time fielding calls from other men for the women they love. He may even cast you an occasional betrayed glance or two.

Be patient with these ill-at-ease feelings. Consider how you would feel if you answered the telephone and an unknown female wanted to speak with your husband or boyfriend. This is a new situation and so it is a hard one to deal with at first, but those uncomfortable looks will soon pass. The man in your life will probably never actually like the idea of you spending time with a male buyer, banker or realtor, but he'll become accustomed to it.

Assess what you want from real estate investing and begin reading up on methods to help you go in that direction. Draw up a list of goals for yourself—what you want from life and what you want from your investments. Establish some priorities and set dates for the accomplishment of your goals. Begin making a daily list of things you need to do. Decide what is the best use of your time, and then do it! Keep your goals and your time line visible.

Be aware that many people will not be as enthusiastic or as positive as you are—they may try to deflate your hopes. Don't allow this. Have confidence in yourself and your abilities and realize that their stories of woe need not be your stories. Take narrow attitudes from anyone, most especially men, with a grain of salt. They are insecure, that's all. Many people are. And be especially gentle and patient with the men in your life. It's tough for them, watching you grow. They fear that you might leave them behind. Assure them that a better financial situation will only improve your relationship and put them at ease.

Learn to take a few risks, and don't be afraid to make a mistake. Remember that very few decisions are irrevocable. If you are fearful—and you likely will be at first—take only small steps until you feel more confident. Most fears are due to a lack of information and knowledge. Educate yourself as much as possible, and then concentrate on what you can accomplish with your newly acquired knowledge.

Goal setters are winners in every phase of life. They are people with a purpose. They have developed self-confidence and the ability to make decisions through their knowledge, goal setting, and doing. Plan your work and work your plan. Be a doer! Be a winner!

CHAPTER THREE

First
Steps

O KAY, LADIES, we're ready for action. You are now prepared to learn about the actual business of real estate investing. We are going to give you some important first steps in this chapter—some essentials to make what is presently dream into reality.

The flow chart shows the necessary steps to building your own investment company. Take a look at it. Notice that you have already accomplished some important tasks by determining your needs and establishing your goals. And by now you are probably feeling more comfortable with the idea of investing in real estate. Just keep telling yourself that you can do it—don't ever let yourself doubt that for even a minute. The most difficult task in any new endeavor is to convince yourself that it is possible. You have already done this. Now for the minor details of finding a good buy, purchasing those houses that are good buys, and renting them for a positive cash flow or selling them for a profit. No problem. Are you ready?

Establishing Credit

A money lender is anyone who is giving you money to buy a house, be this person a banker, an employee at a mortgage company, or an officer at a loan association. Even if you make it a policy to always buy owner-financed properties, you are dealing with a lender—the owner himself is indirectly lending you money so you can buy that home. Any individual offering owner financing will likely insist on a credit report on you (*we* always do a credit check on prospective buyers—it would be far too risky not to).

Your Path to Real Estate Investing

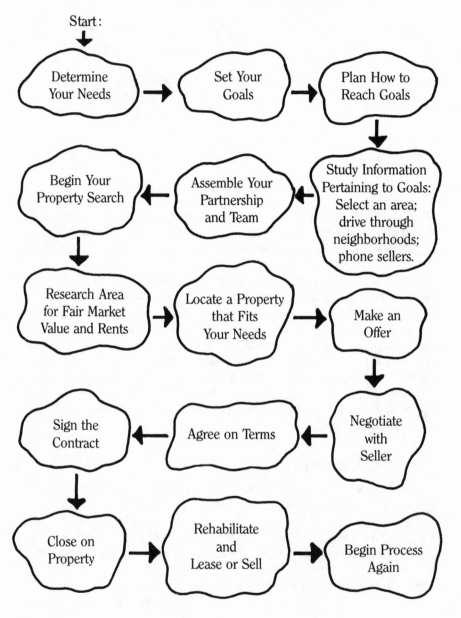

Start:

Determine Your Needs → Set Your Goals → Plan How to Reach Goals

Begin Your Property Search ← Assemble Your Partnership and Team ← Study Information Pertaining to Goals: Select an area; drive through neighborhoods; phone sellers.

Research Area for Fair Market Value and Rents → Locate a Property that Fits Your Needs → Make an Offer

Sign the Contract ← Agree on Terms ← Negotiate with Seller

Close on Property → Rehabilitate and Lease or Sell → Begin Process Again

Anyone who lends you money will usually be slightly wary of all those he comes in contact with (you would be, too, if others were always asking you for money). You want to make these people feel secure in your presence. You can do this. Improve your credit rating and loan officers and other money lenders will do more than feel secure—they will become as friendly as your closest pals. Sound difficult? Not with a patient and careful approach.

Keep in mind that when we talk about credit rating, we mean literally *your* credit rating, not your husband's, boyfriend's, or parents'. If you are married and are going into real estate investing on your own, or with someone other than your husband, it is essential that you have your *own* credit rating. Perhaps you had the foresight to keep some credit items (car purchase, house or rent payments, etc.) in your own name and already have a good credit rating, or maybe you have a personal friend who is a banker, and he realizes you can meet any payment on time. Whatever the cause of your healthy credit rating, if you feel that it needs no more help, you may want to skip over this section.

Your first task, for those of you ladies who need help with your credit rating, is to find out what you're up against. You need to run a credit check on yourself. This is an easy process that will show you what needs to be done to improve (or establish) a good credit rating.

In your city or state, it is probably as easy and inexpensive for you to get a credit report as it is for us in our own community. Check in your telephone directory—you will find a listing for credit bureaus there. Try the yellow pages under "credit bureaus" or "credit reporting," and then you should be on the right track. Start making calls. Find out what you need to do to get a credit report. This will probably entail a fee of five to ten dollars. Your report may take a couple of days, unless you go in for a personal review of it—in that case, you could possibly get a report the same day.

Later, you may want to go ahead and join a credit bureau. When renting and selling houses in the future, a credit bureau speeds up the process of finding out whether your prospective tenant or buyer has paid his bills on time. This usually involves a monthly fee, but it is well worth it. Ask the credit bureau you have chosen about its terms, and remember—shop around.

But stop! Supposing the credit bureau has never heard of you, or worse, perhaps they have heard something nasty about you. Never fear. We have not left you behind. There is something to be done to make it look more acceptable to those in banker's gray.

Before you begin moving with your credit rating improvement, make certain that what it says about you is correct. We three have at least once each discovered via a credit report that we have debts for things we never knew we had bought. It's a shock to find out you own a camper that you've never seen, and even more heartstopping to find that you're eight months behind in your payments on it!

Carol recalls once visiting a lender who was very slow in qualifying her for a loan. Much to her dismay, the lender told her that she had declared bankruptcy! Carol was beside herself. How could such an error be on the credit report? How long had it been there? The report was corrected as fast as Carol could dial the phone!

Keep in mind that computers make mistakes, and make sure no computer has made up myths about your money situation. Such mistakes are usually remedied by a few telephone calls. If you have a name that somebody else might be sharing (as in Carol A. Wilson), use your full middle name and your social security number on any loan application (it is a good idea to use your social security number on any important document, even if your name is Desidera Quinn Obradovich. You never know when another might move into town).

Also, be sure that your credit report has all of your credit pluses on it. Landlords and creditors are always quick to report bad bill-paying habits, but they often neglect to say good things about you. For instance, if in the past you rented an apartment and paid those bills promptly but this doesn't show up on your credit report, give your former landlord a call and ask if he is willing to send you a letter verifying those punctual payments. If he is pleasant, ask him to send a copy off to the credit bureau too. Call up any mortgage or finance company or bank that you have paid promptly and ask for a letter from them also. Keep these letters with your financial statement to show to anyone who you are hoping to impress with your financial efficiency.

But suppose you either don't have a credit rating, or it is an unacceptable one and there is no one to call to make it look any better. Still, there are ways to improve this situation.

Are you going past a big department store today? The kind that sells everything from baby carriages to power tools? Go in and fill out a credit card application. They will likely be very happy to see you; they might even give you a liter of your favorite soft drink, a pair of sunglasses, and a small dog just for filling out one of their applications. Big department stores are not so picky about whom they give credit cards because they're not risking as much as major credit cards companies are.

Once you get a department store credit card, use it. Purchase that new screwdriver set you were going to buy anyway, or take the kids shopping for some new shoes. The *moment* you get the bill for your purchases, pay it. And then go do it again. Perhaps you have been planning on buying a lawn mower for two summers and you finally have the money to do it—now is the time to get it and you know the place to purchase it. You can pay for it slowly, if you choose, but remember those credit charges.

Do you see what you've done? You have just improved your credit rating. Prompt payments go down on your report for all future creditors to see.

If you have something negative on your credit report, now is the time to fix it. You didn't pay your dentist bill from two years ago? Maybe you forgot and just kept forgetting as his reminders came in every month. Well, pay it off now. Perhaps you don't have enough money to do it in one lump sum. This is no excuse to let a real estate investment career pass you by. Call up the firm you offended by not paying your bills and explain that you would like to pay your bills but cannot do it in one quick payment. Set up some sort of payment per month and *keep with those payments.* They will agree to do this. Do not be nervous and do not waste time by feeling embarrassed. Remember that those to whom you owe money are as anxious to get the debt paid off as you are to clear your credit rating. They want their money and are willing to bend to do it. Any business that you owe will do this, be it the telephone company, the electric company, or whatever. Negotiate—that's what we women are good at. If you have many such bills, it may take some time to improve the way you look to creditors, so get started today. Once you get your credit rating looking a bit better, use the techniques we have outlined here for the woman who has no credit rating.

Other things will improve your credit rating. For instance, go to the bank where your savings and checking accounts are and ask about loan possibilities. If your institution does not offer personal loans, find one that does. Move your accounts there if you have to. And then apply for a loan. It doesn't have to be for much—$500 will look nice enough (make sure there is no pre-payment penalty before you sign anything). Once you get that money, put it into your savings and *don't use it.* Make two or three payments on it, and then withdraw that money from your savings and pay the entire loan off. Do it again, this time with more money. Loans that are paid off before they are due look very nice to nervous loan officers. And the only fee you are paying is the interest payment for the few months you have the loan; for this small amount, you have just made yourself look much better to those who might otherwise consider you a credit risk.

Eventually you're going to want to apply for a major credit card. If you have taken the steps we've outlined for you, it should be easier to get one. With this credit card you can continue bettering your credit rating. Just remember those twenty percent credit charges and pay your bills on time.

A note to any woman who may have a bankruptcy or foreclosure on her record and is trying to bounce back: Do not give up. If you've mended your ways, you deserve a chance to try again. It may take a few years for such black marks to be erased. If that period has not elapsed yet, there is still a way into real estate investing in the meantime. Find a partner or a person with good credit to cosign with you. You may have to do more of the legwork since you are contributing no money to the partnership, but this is better than waiting for seven years to crawl by.

Once you have done this, you need to prepare a financial statement, which you can do by simply typing one out or by picking up a financial statement form from the lending institution. In your statement you need to put all of your assets and liabilities, your valuables, the loans that you have taken out, etc. Put down addresses of people with whom you have established your credit. This collection of facts will tell a lender bank what you are worth and whether or not you're a good credit risk.

Once you have your credit rating and your financial statement, you're ready to apply for a loan or alternate financing plan. (Don't let the word financing scare you—we have included a chapter to explain it to you.)

A healthy credit rating is invaluable to your investing career. It will also make buying any expensive item an easier process. Spend some time with your credit rating, and watch every business transaction you make become easier to complete. Once your credit rating looks virtuous and strong, keep it that way. No one likes to pay bills, even if he or she has ample money. Don't procrastinate! Remember that you are now in a business where your credit report is your most important asset.

Getting on with Business

At this point, you want to familiarize yourself more with the home-buying process. A good way is by reading your local daily newspaper. If you live in a large city, there are probably a couple of pages of ads listing houses for sale in each paper. Go over those ads. You'll see some odd terms and abbreviations. Don't worry about that—turn to our glossary in the back, find out what those weird terms mean, and continue to familiarize yourself with real estate. If there is a specific real estate section in the paper, take a look at it. Read the articles. You'll find stories about the latest trends in real estate, the availability of loans, and many other useful things. Don't do anything with what you learn from these articles; just learn, and keep the information for future reference. You may want to subscribe to a small, local paper at this point if you are interested in going after bargain homes via public auctions. Call your county courthouse and find out which papers publish their announcements of impending public trustee (foreclosure) and sheriff sales. Take a look at those announcements. This can be a good learning process.

You will need to begin learning the different areas of your city. Start by driving around areas close to your neighborhood. What do the houses look like? Do you feel safe in these neighborhoods? What kind of people seem to live there? Would you like to own a rental property in this neighborhood? How far is it from your home? (While you are doing this, make sure to record your mileage, date, etc. Remember that in your new business, this is a deduction.)

Eventually you will find an area of town in which you are going to start working. For a beginning woman investor, we would recommend that you choose an area that is reasonably priced (leave investing in mansions as a future project), allows rentals (watch the zoning!), is within half an hour from your home, and is safe. It is vital that it be a *safe* area. You want to feel comfortable going there alone or after dark; if you have children, you want to feel good about letting them play in the backyard.

Keep an eye out for those "for sale" signs, whether they are by owner or a real estate company. Are there many of them in a certain neighborhood? If so, it could be that those properties are priced too high. If you are feeling confident, go talk to the owner with a "for sale by owner" sign out front. What is he asking for the house? Has he any idea why so many houses are up for sale? (This last could reveal much—maybe there is good reason people are leaving in droves: proximity to a nuclear waste dump, frequency of volcanic eruptions, etc. You probably would be better off to continue looking in this case.) Learn to like owners who are selling their homes themselves—you will soon be working with them regularly.

Now is a good time to start making calls on properties. Do it for practice only—you just want to know what it's like. You'll find it's very simple and there is no obligation involved. We have included a list of questions that we ask people who are selling their home (see the chapter on buying your first home). Take a look at those questions and throw a couple of them at the home owner. It's not that tough, is it? Are you feeling those first thrills of bargain hunting for homes? This is far more exhilarating than looking for a nice melon, believe us! And it gets better. At this time you may want to talk with a real estate salesperson. Go into his or her office and gather all of the information you can find there. Explain that you want to begin buying investment properties and are looking for an agent to work with. Ask about rent and home values in the area in which you are considering buying, and about any low priced houses he or she may be aware of. Take a look at the Multiple Listing Books. If the two of you get along well, you may even go out to look at houses together. Ask where you can get an amortization book (this is simply a book that has a listing of different monthly payments on differently priced homes at different interest rates). You may just get one.

Since we're talking about real estate salesmen, this might be a good time to consider whether or not you should get your own license to sell real estate. Many people ask us whether we have real estate licenses. Not one of us does. We each considered getting one but we decided not to, even though such training could only have helped us understand more of the field. We chose not to get licenses for several reasons, the most important of which is: if you have a real estate license, you must tell that to a seller or buyer before any transaction can take place. This is a law. And many buyers and sellers are wary of a real estate salesperson. Not that real estate salespeople are not nice guys—they usually are—but people don't trust them as much as they do three former school teachers turned investors. Sellers tend to think that salespeople know more than they do and thus can be unwilling to talk to an agent. The other reason we did not get licenses is that no one needs a license to sell or buy real estate. We now feel we know as much as a typical beginning real estate salesperson does about the field, and yet we're received more warmly by buyers and sellers (and we saved ourselves some money on the examination fees).

Also keep in mind when debating the advantages of a license that if you have one, you will be expected to know more about real estate laws and will receive much more attention from your state's real estate regulatory agencies.

To further familiarize yourself with the home-buying process, you may want to go out to your county courthouse and look up some titles to properties. First call and see what hours the records room is open. Once you arrive, ask one of the clerks to help you look up a title (they are usually kept on microfilm rolls). Watch carefully what she does and the next time you probably won't need her help.

Most likely there will be signs in this room that warn you to get the advice of an attorney on any title questions you may have. These signs are there for a reason. We are by no means recommending that you look up a title on a house and decide to buy it on your own judgment. We always use a title insurance company before buying a home, and consult a lawyer with any legal questions we have. We advise you to do the same. But there is some value to this lesson at the courthouse: it familiarizes you with titles and thus leaves you more comfortable with them.

Now you're getting somewhere. Up until now, you have only put time into this idea—if you still feel good about it, let's start putting some money into it.

You're going to need some paper items, namely business cards and stationery. Perhaps you have an idea in mind for a catchy graphic or saying on your card? Now is the time to take that idea to a graphic artist and get it made up into a design you can put on your cards and letters. We had a design made up that we have put on our cards, stationery, and "For sale" signs. A copy shop might be able to make up both your design and business cards. Remember to shop prices! It applies in this as in all else.

Call up business supply stores and ask whether they carry real estate contracts. You could buy some of these, or you could consult a lawyer and draw up your own. Make sure you have a contingency clause in your contract (a contingency clause is simply a written passage which states that any deal is contingent upon a certain condition—it is an escape route in case you bite into a rotten apple). A lawyer can advise you on how to word this.

A good buy at this time is a message recorder to attach to your phone. This, unfortunately, is not cheap; it will probably cost a couple hundred dollars, thus proving to be the most costly investment yet in your investing career. You will probably not need it right away, so if you would rather pay for it with your first profits, that's fine. Just remember that you'll need one eventually. You do not want to miss any calls that could bring in money for you, do you? That couple hundred you spend will quickly be made up if just one message makes it to you and creates a sale. Put some sort of persuasive recording on that leaves people more liable to leave a number. And always return your calls! Even if something seems unimportant, it just might make or save you some money.

Speaking of recorders, there was one particular incident that made Lynda decide it was time to spring for a telephone recording device. Lynda's sons were notorious for not taking messages well. One message which they failed to give her was a realtor calling with a package of two houses for a very low price, a message which could have cost us a $30,000 profit if the realtor hadn't taken the incentive to phone when his previous calls were not returned. No telling what other buys we might have missed. Those messages can be worth thousands. You may also want to buy yourself a calculator, or ask for one for Christmas. This way you can quickly figure payments, profit margins, and other important numbers. This is not something you need right away—or ever, for that matter—but if you have a difficult time with numbers, it makes them much less intimidating. The three of us have one we use when figuring the interest rate or present value of a property. They are a little confusing at first, but if you devote an hour to learning how to use your calculator, it will certainly be an hour well spent.

There is one last item we think you should buy for your new business—a photo scrapbook. We bought one before purchasing our first properties and we think it's a great idea. You will also need a camera—not an elaborate one; an instamatic will do. When we buy a home, any home, Carol takes several pictures of the house for us. We almost always try to get pictures of ourselves in these photos, along with the house. We don't do this so we can look back nostalgically at the pictures—we do it to prove to others, most especially those from whom we're trying to receive a loan, that we are serious investors and successful in our business. No doubt you've seen this sort of approach in magazines and newspapers.

Pick up any woman's magazine and you will find at least one advertisement that uses the before-and-after method of convincing you to buy their product. These ads are very effective; a rather plain woman becomes gorgeous after using some sort of makeup, cologne, or diet. We are advertising something too—our business. We're showing anyone who picks up that scrapbook that we have the ability to make a lovely home out of a hovel. We have pictures of ourselves actually doing the work, which should prove to any doubtful male that women are capable of accomplishing any task. We also have included in the scrapbook newspaper articles published about us.

Once, the scrapbook was very valuable to someone besides our banker. We needed a small city's support before we could receive a federal grant for renovation on a housing project for the elderly. To go in unknown and simply ask for its support probably would not have gotten us anywhere, but with our scrapbook, we were able to prove we were equal to the job at hand. The city gave us its support and approval to receive the federal loan. So get a scrapbook and be prepared to start taking pictures of your achievements with your homes. You never know when it will be valuable.

Of course, anything you buy for your new career is a business expense.

Remember this and save all your receipts for payments that pertain to your investments, whether it's a can of paint or the fee you pay your lawyer for drawing up your partnership agreement. Keep these receipts in a safe place so that you can deduct them as a business expense come tax time. This is why we told you to record your mileage before—you can deduct it too. Your accountant will need to see everything (see our record-keeping chapter for more information).

Get the Word Out!

Your new business is really starting to take form, isn't it? You already have the basic materials to get going. Now you need to let people—as many of them as possible—know what you are up to. You have your business cards? Don't just leave them in your pocketbook or use them as bookmarks—others need to see them! If you are at the grocery store, leave one on the announcement board. Put them on bulletin boards anywhere you see them. Give them to people you meet. And make a point of telling people what you do for a living. Tell your relatives! Have your family spread the word. We once made a great buy because one of our husbands told the people he worked with that his wife was in an investment partnership that buys homes. One of his co-workers needed to sell his house very badly and was willing to sell it for far below market price. As soon as we heard his situation, we gave him an offer on his house. We helped him and he helped us, which is why we're in this business. If he hadn't known that we buy homes, we would have lost a good buy.

Use your business stationery for letters you write (not all of them—unless you want to be especially cold and cruel, write any Dear John letters on something else). Any business letter should, of course, be on your stationery, but you can use it for other correspondence as well. Perhaps you're going on vacation and need to tell the milkman about it? Write him a quick note on that valuable stationery. Making a donation to someone? Put your accompanying note on your paper with its informative letterhead and mail it in your business envelope. All this helps get the word around that you like to buy homes.

Some investors advise printing flyers and distributing them in all parts of town (we had our kids do this for us). Sure, some people will wad them up and throw them away without even looking at them. But, by the law of averages, some will read those flyers with your phone number on them and give you a call. Maybe that call will not make you a dime, but one day those flyers will bring you some business, either directly or indirectly, and what you paid to print them will certainly be worth it. Post a few on telephone poles or street signs next to garage sale announcements. Don't post your flyers without permission, however, since it may be against one of your city's ordinances.

Try putting an ad in the paper. It doesn't have to be an elaborate ad—just something good enough to get people's attention. This is effective: *I'll buy your house.* Add your telephone number and you'll eventually get some calls. You could get a lot of calls; it just depends on how many people are looking to sell their homes and how desperate they are.

By informing as many people as possible that you are in the investing business, you're playing the averages. The more people who know about it, the more people who are likely to give you a call if they need to sell their house in a hurry. Perhaps a true "don't-wanter" hears from his second cousin's next-door neighbor that she has an acquaintance who knows a woman who buys homes as an investment. This don't-wanter will probably take some steps to find out how he can speak with you. Believe us, the grapevine works.

You may also want to join a real estate investment group. Call up a couple of real estate offices to find out if they know where one meets. With such a group, you can learn more about the business of investing, get advice when you need it, and perhaps even drum up some business. It also makes you feel more at ease to be around other people doing the same thing you are. You'll make some new friends. If you are just going into the field and need to find a partner, this could be the place to start your search. Even if you don't join, go to a meeting. They will not refuse you, and it's a learning experience. We have always been treated most cordially by our investment group. Yes, they are mostly men, but they're usually nice men who will welcome you.

We hope the information in this chapter has helped you a bit. If you're still feeling uncertain, don't worry. Just keep acquiring knowledge, and those uneasy feelings will soon go away, especially after you have bought your first home.

CHAPTER FOUR

Partnerships

HAVE YOU EVER BEEN to a picnic and watched a group of ants take a piece of cake across your picnic table, down the leg, and head off for their ant hill? Consider what these ants seem to know intuitively. Any difficult task is made easier by sharing it with someone else.

One of the most important aspects of real estate investing is your status when you go into the business: Will you do all this alone, or will you take on one or more partners?

We three did not want to jump into an investment career alone. It's a great responsibility to start and then run your own company, and none of us wanted to take on this responsibility without the mental support that partners can offer. The fact that we decided to go into business together has worked out well for us, but you need to consider your own situation before deciding on whether to seek a partner.

First let's deal with the adverse aspects of having a partner. The most obvious reason not to has to do with money. With any sort of partner you are expected to share things; with a partner in any business, you're expected to share your *profits*. If you share your profits with someone, you can count on it taking twice as long to become independently wealthy than it otherwise would. You will, of course, have to work much harder without a business buddy to help you, but you might become a real estate tycoon faster.

If you're a person who craves solitude, you may not want a partner. Perhaps you work more efficiently without another person around. If this is your disposition, be aware that you are apt to spend quite a bit of time with your partner, and if you work better alone, you might do better without one.

Qualifying for a loan is more difficult in partnership than if you are alone (but it is by no means impossible!). In our case, the lender has to qualify three people instead of one. Having a partner can work to your advantage if one has money and another doesn't, but if you all insist on taking equal parts of the financial burden and want to get a loan as a single entity, it will take longer to process the forms. Sometimes, by the time your loan is approved, the seller may have had to change his closing date several times. A lender might reject your loan application simply because for the same amount of time he could put through three loans. This is his job, remember—to put through as many loans as possible.

There are time delays in a partnership because of decisions that must be made. Decisions cannot be made as quickly as when one person is running the entire show. We spend many hours on the phone giving our various opinions on any issue. Three-way calling helps cut delays in our decision-making process, but if you are a person who likes to make quick assessments and find solutions promptly, you may do better with a silent partner or without one at all.

These are some of the negative aspects to having a partner, but for us the positive aspects far outweigh the negative. All three of us agree that if we had to do it over again, we would go the partner route. We do have to share profits, but we also share work, good times and bad times.

When your tenant calls with frozen pipes, it is nice to have a partner to share the burden. It is also more fun depositing that big check when you're not alone at the bank window.

We have been very lucky in our partnership. When the three of us went to that seminar three years ago, it was the beginning of a very successful business relationship. While we three were well suited for a real estate career together, separately we might not have been as successful. Each minor stumbling block might have been overwhelming to one of us, but with three, we talked each other through the scary moments.

Also, we complement each other perfectly for this field by having our own special skills. Everybody has strengths and talents, but in this field you need a whole range of varied talents that one personality is not likely to have.

You need to be a good shopper, a creative decorator, and a willing worker. You need patience and mechanical ability. You need a sense of humor and fairness. Add to this an optimistic and positive attitude with lots of self-discipline and drive, and you get an idea of the various talents needed to get a real estate investing business off the ground. How many people possess all of these traits? We have said that women are likely to have most of these varied talents, but a woman by herself is not going to have all of them. Why do you think big businesses and successful partnerships have so many people working for them? Because different people have different strengths.

In our partnership, for example, Jane is a whiz with numbers and makes an excellent bookkeeper. She can figure numbers in her head faster than Carol and Lynda can find their calculators. She can rapidly calculate while talking to an owner or agent whether what she is hearing is a profitable endeavor or not. As a speedy thinker, Jane comes up with solutions to problems very quickly.

Carol is extremely confident; our public relations person, a tough negotiator. She is ready and willing to take on any project because she knows she can do it. She is a very positive person who has not had a negative thought in a long, long time. She is also very mechanical. She can fix things—plumbing, electrical, and mechanical problems are a snap for her. This is a natural ability on her part that the other two just were not born with.

Lynda is compassionate and has a perceptive nature. She is our arbitrator and psychologist. She analyzes any problems and soothes any ruffled feelings, whether these ruffled feelings are felt by a buyer, seller, banker, or workman. When we're having disagreements within the partnership, she has the ability to remain unperturbed, and makes our operation work far more smoothly by making impartial judgments. She can perceive the needs of a buyer, and develop a deal that he will be likely to accept. This is a vital part of negotiations, and it is a skill that many women possess.

Because of our different abilities, any of us on our own would probably not be doing as well alone as we are working together. Also, putting aside the securing of loans we mentioned before, there are things that teams get done more quickly than single players. For example, when we take over a house it does not take us very long to get going with the rehabilitation process because we have the drive and self-discipline of three people pushing to get the job done instead of one. Three people, or however many are in your partnership, are not so likely to procrastinate as one person alone.

Speaking of rehabs, they are much easier to get through with a partner by your side. Going into a house in which each room needs to be cleaned from ceiling to floor is much easier when you can divide the work by two or three. Each of us only needs to clean every third toilet! That, it often seems, is reason enough to get a partner, since some of the homes we have bought have been downright filthy (that's why we got them for bargain rates).

And remember, cockroaches and dead snakes can be funny when there are others to share your horror. We once found a dead snake in a cabinet in one of our rehabs. After the initial shock and terror about whether it was alive or not, we calmed down and began to laugh. We laughed and laughed and then scattered in three directions to get a broom, a sack, and a camera. We put a picture in our scrapbook to show anyone who looks through it that even snakes will not deter us. We have had some of our funniest and best moments while working on our homes, and we have built a great friendship. A successful business, a great partnership, financial and personal freedom, and three very good friends—that's what wealth and prosperity should be all about.

Having a partner also makes redecorating more enjoyable. We discuss cleaning and decorating strategies together before we go to work. We can paint a house in a single day, and have become the fastest wallpapering team east of the Rockies. One measures and cuts, the other pastes, and the third hangs it on the wall. We can usually finish a room with plenty of time to go to lunch. We also have found that we get a lot of decisions made when we're painting a room together. Who says that a business meeting can't take place with paintbrush in hand or while scrubbing and dusting?

With a partner, you can allocate different tasks to each, and spend your time more economically. That is extremely important to all three of us; we have more time to spend at leisure. We can also avoid repeatedly doing the loathsome jobs that we despise. Say, for instance, that you detest any sort of bookkeeping but your partner can deal with it happily enough. She doesn't like to do any lawn work at all, though, and this happens to be your forte. Your partner can do the bookkeeping and you can do the lawn work. If you feel very strongly about the tasks that you insist on either doing or not doing, you can address these issues in your partnership agreement. If you were alone, you would have no choice but to do everything yourself, or pay a fee to have them done for you.

We find that we are much less intimidated by the business world when we approach it as a team—three heads are definitely better than one in a negotiating session. We make a formidable group, unintimidated by the buyers or businessmen across the table from us.

After the seller has recuperated from the fact that he is seated across the table from three women investors, we hit him with our well-rehearsed plan. Jane begins the negotiations by presenting the numbers portion of the offer. She finds out what the seller's needs are and tries to adjust those numbers to accomodate both parties. When the negotiating session comes to a point where no one is giving, Lynda comes in with, "I know we can work this out," or, "Surely there is some way we can meet both of our needs here." The seller is usually willing to talk again. When we have given as much as we care to, Carol steps in. "Nope," she says. "That's it." She stands firm. If neither party can compromise any more, then we walk away from those negotiations. But more often than not, we're able to come to a mutually satisfying agreement.

Having a partner may give you strength when you need it. When you are down and out and ready to quit, your partner can help pull you through. If a certain task is too scary to do alone— for women, going into certain neighborhoods alone, delivering eviction notices, etc., can be unnerving—you can double up. Few situations are so intimidating that they cannot be handled together. Also, important details are not as likely to be forgotten when there is more than one brain trying to remember, and with more than one pair of eyes looking, your partnership sees more, whether it's a leaky ceiling or a profitable solution.

Having a partner adds even more to the flexibility you have by being your own boss. If on some gloomy day you wake up and find that you're not well at all, you have the option of calling your partner between sneezes and giving up your responsibilities for the day. Then, instead of braving that gray and unappealing world, you can crawl back into bed and shiver and shake in the privacy of your own room. You won't be feeling miserable, and inflicting your sickness on everyone you have to meet. The business continues in your absence.

What to look for in a Partner

Before considering a partner, you need to perform some more self-assessment. Each of us has her own strengths and weaknesses and these need to be dealt with before you can pick a partner who will complement your talents and abilities.

You should first be aware of what you can tolerate: know what drives you crazy. If you are an early riser who simply must have eight things done by eight, you'd do well to avoid going into a partnership with someone who can't think before noon. Jane's mind clicks on anywhere before four and five. She runs down shortly after lunch. Lynda and Carol click on at a more normal hour, seven, and can usually last until four. We try to schedule any important negotiating when we are fresh. For another example: If you are fastidiously accurate in your record keeping, stay away from the person who has only a vague idea where his income tax returns and insurance documents are. Such conflicts in character could lead to a disastrous partnership.

Be aware of what your general goals are. Does your prospective partner have any goals? What are they? If she simply wants to make enough so she can move to an African village and learn to speak Swahili fluently, she may not be the person for you. If one of you is going into investing for the tax advantages, and the other needs some quick money for the dress boutique she wants to open next year, then there might already be some seeds of contention. You need to have similar drives and complimentary dispositions. You are going to be in a relationship with this person that is second only to marriage; you will be tied together legally and financially and spending countless hours in each other's company. So that you do not have to go through a messy and stressful "divorce" later on, be selective.

You also should keep in mind the demands that are placed on you by others. If you are married with three children, to become a partner with a single person could be a mistake. She might not understand why you must go to parents' conferences and kids' Christmas shows. You might be better off working with someone who has the same type of family commitments as you do. You need to both be willing and able to give the same amount of time to investing. If you are not able to work weekends and only want to work two late nights a month, make sure your partner knows this before you sign any agreements, so the two of you can come to a compromise.

We are not saying that you should be exactly like your partner— far from it. You need diverse talents in real estate investing. But you need to have some common ground or it leads to tense relationships. Compromise is always possible, but if you start out with semi-equal needs and time to give to the business, it will move more smoothly.

Consider what your talents are. Are you a whiz with numbers or people? Are you a shrewd businesswoman or hopelessly naive and unable to negotiate well? If you are a shy person, you will do better if you can find someone more gregarious than yourself. Many situations require plain old guts, and so if you are timid, it would be a good idea to find a more forceful partner. One of you will have to be an organized person who can tolerate and efficiently do paperwork. If this is not your strength, find a partner who loves detail. Basically, you should find someone you can get along with and who has the traits that you do not. Your partnership will be more likely to succeed with such a person, and thus your new venture will be more profitable. Remember, a good partnership needs constant work, just like a good marriage.

One of the reasons that our partnership has been so successful is that we all choose to devote at least forty hours a week to it. This is not all hard work;

we find it entertaining to go house shopping, and it is especially fun to pick up checks for large amounts at closings. But this, no matter how much fun we have, is our job. We never let a day go by without accomplishing something in our business and for our partnership. Some days are slower than others; we may do nothing more than drive by our properties and check the maintenance or call banks to inquire whether they have any foreclosures they're trying to sell. But none of us tries to avoid our work. You need partners who have this attitude. If a person is not willing to work hard, you would best pass her by.

You should also determine whether your partner is willing to do the physical work on a house or if she would prefer to hire someone to do such jobs. Some women would rather endure torture than clean a house.

We should mention here that, in our opinion, we have found partnerships involving women usually work better than those between men. Due to our society's demands from men, they tend to be more aggressive and are not as likely as women to try to come to a reasonable solution if a problem comes up in the partnership. Men are often quick to walk away. We were told by several men when we first started that we should not get involved in a partnership because it would lead to the end of our friendship, and failure. They were basing this advice on their own past experiences. Men do have problems with partnerships, but as women, we have been taught all our lives that our role is to give, so we are more willing to give and share equally. A woman usually works harder to make a romantic relationship work, because she is more communicative. Communication makes a partnership work as well. In our case, we all wanted so desperately for our business to succeed that we were willing to put in a great deal of effort to see that our partnership succeeded.

Just keep in mind that whether you are sharing the sorrows of frozen water pipes on a cold January morning, or the joy of your latest profit, it is nice to be learning and growing with another person (or persons!).

If working with another person day in and day out does not appeal to you, but you still need the financial support a partner offers, remember that there is another type of partner for you to consider: the silent partner. This person may just not have the time or strength (perhaps he or she is handicapped in some way) to do the legwork necessary for successful investing. Maybe your silent partner just wants the tax benefits that you can provide if he or she helps finance your buys.

Once you have decided to put together your efforts with another person, you must draw up a partnership agreement. You do not have to do this immediately, but if you don't sign an agreement *before* you invest, postponing the formality for a future date, you may well regret it. No matter how close your friendship with your partner right now, that friendship could be destroyed in the event that he or she wanted to leave the partnership and you had no legal parameters to guide you. You want to know where you stand, and a partnership agreement will do this for you. Agree on what the two of you want the agreement to say—and make these decisions when you are both in a good mood and things are going well. Consider possible situations, such as what you would do in the event of the death or disability of a partner. Then consult a lawyer. (Make sure to call beforehand and ask his fee. Otherwise, you may be hit with a bill that will give you heart failure.) So stay friends and stay legal—spend some money on a bona fide agreement.

Partnerships with Men

Maybe some of you ladies are considering throwing your talents in with a man as you step into real estate investing. We think this is an excellent idea. Whether he is your husband (see next section), boyfriend, an old friend, or someone you just met at a real estate seminar, a man-woman team could be the ultimate combination in this field. Consider it. All the talents he doesn't have, you *do* have. He can give you strength and support. You can give him shopping, negotiating, and decorating ability. He can perhaps give you more knowledge of the business world; you can give him budgeting and organizational skills. You can both clean and fix up a property together, and all the while be learning from one another. Women often have intuition men do not possess, giving them a far more perceptive nature. Women are more likely to try to keep a partnership going during rough times. For any man who happens to be reading this book, we think that the smartest thing you could do this week is pick a woman as your partner.

Husband and Wife Teams

Because so many women are considering investing with their husbands, we have decided to include a section specifically concerning such a team.

Many of the women we see at seminars are there with their husbands. We think this is great—a real estate investing partnership adds to the marital partnership that is already going strong. The financial security that buying real estate investment properties provides adds much to a marriage; it gives you opportunities that you just do not have with other jobs. To do all this *together* would be very rewarding for both the husband and wife.

What you must avoid, though, is a partnership that falls prey to stereotyped roles. You should both keep in mind that if the woman ends up with all of the jobs that typically are given to a woman, the partnership could quickly sour. Nor should a woman leave all the decisions to the man. You have a chance here to build a very successful team—do not mess it up by reverting to unproductive roles.

No woman is going to be happy watching her husband charging ahead without her into real estate investing; it makes her feel all the more like a maid. While he's using his mind creatively and building a successful and interesting career, she is still home cleaning or caring for the kids. He is the first adult she has seen all day when he walks in at night, and she is tired, beat, and disillusioned with her role in life. Her husband is feeling good about himself when he returns home; she feels like a leftover zero. She will end up resenting his outside interests; he will not comprehend why she is distant. Maybe she is still at a dead-end job, watching him blast off. By the time the husband finds his first property, the wife has just about had it. She did not participate in the shopping, negotiating, or planning, but now her husband would like some help with cleaning. Why shouldn't she be smoldering? Now she has *two* houses to clean. A marriage could even drift apart if some consideration is not given the woman.

As we have stressed repeatedly in this chapter, you need to keep in mind strengths and weaknesses. Maybe the husband is happy doing the calling and the wife would rather drive through the neighborhoods. If the wife is better with people, she should be working with people. If the husband can put up wallpaper more efficiently, then he should be doing that. It is the same with any other partnership—do what you do best.

If the man has a full-time job that he cannot quit abruptly to jump into an investment career, his wife—if she is not working—could lay the groundwork. She could do the ad searching, make the calls, and wander the neighborhoods with the kids. If she is working, both husband and wife could work together during off-hours to get themselves started.

We advise a couple just entering the real estate investing world to do all of their learning together. Attend seminars together, read your books together, and listen to your tapes together. By learning side by side, you will be able to share the excitement about your prospects at the same time and neither will be resenting the other's newfound interest. You should take great care to progress at the same rate. If one of you gets ahead of the other, it is easy to leave that one behind; take the time to help him or her catch up.

If the two of you are planning on going in together but you can only afford one seminar price, we advise that the woman go. This is not out of deference to our own sex, but because we realize that most men know more about the process of buying a house than a woman does. She usually lets him sign the papers and do the business work. It is time for the two of you to work together—let her catch up first, and then start really jumping ahead. Stay on an equal footing. We have called many times on properties and asked the woman questions to which she doesn't have answers. Her response? " You'll have to call back when my husband is here—he knows the numbers, I don't." She has just lost a deal if we don't call back.

So, start on equal ground together, and work on equal ground to make real estate investing work for you. If you are going into this with your husband, have him read a few chapters of this book. You are a natural in the field of real estate investing; you are the ingredient that could make this new dish the two of you are cooking really turn out well. Learn together and work together—you have so much going for you both.

CHAPTER FIVE

People on Your Team

HAVE YOU EVER NOTICED when watching a football game that a great quarterback is usually not successful unless he has expert support personnel on his team? If the guard doesn't do his job, even the greatest quarterback is going to be in trouble. Consider yourself the quarterback and begin searching for other individuals you will need as part of your team. You do not need to assemble these team members immediately, but you will eventually need to enlist their services, so you should keep your ears and eyes open for someone who might be able to fill your needs.

Before we describe the others who will benefit the team, we would like to remind you that none of these team members are permanent. If you're ever dissatisfied with their services (the services for which you are paying), you can sever your relationship with them. These individuals are not as important to you as your partner is, so, if you make an error in your choice of team members, you can change your mind. An efficient, dependable team behind you can make your investment career move more smoothly toward success, and may eliminate many headaches.

Real Estate Agents: Pros and Cons

The first team member you may deal with is a real estate agent. You must decide whether you're going to use an agent or not, and, if you are, what your business relationship will be with him or her. It may be surprising to learn that you do not need to use the services of a licensed real estate agent. We have not always used agents, and we've made marvelous and perfectly legal deals. You can do the same thing. We do, however, have an agent who helps us in many of our purchases. She is extremely valuable to us, and has eased us through many buys with a lot less hassle than we might have had otherwise.

There are pros and cons to working with an agent, just as there are advantages and disadvantages to having a partner. Whether you choose to use an agent or to sell your property yourself depends largely on your personal needs and the things you're willing to give up to make a sale. For example, your time. Your time might be too valuable to you for you to work your way through the paperwork of every deal yourself. As we have mentioned before, you earn your money when you purchase your property—but you don't pocket your profit until you sell. If an agent will help you sell, by all means, use an agent.

Real estate agents have immense pools of knowledge to offer. They also have access to Multiple Listing Books that are not available to the unlicensed investor. Further, they have joined the computer age, and can utilize those wonderful machines to narrow down the otherwise immense market that you must search, according to important factors such as area, available financing, and price range. If they are looking for bargains for you, they can check their listings every day and find out about listings before they come out in the MLS books, thus allowing you to deal with less competition and take advantage of the first choice of properties.

Let's say, for example, that your desired purchase is a home with a non-qualifying, assumable mortgage at a rate of less than ten percent. You want to purchase that home for under $50,000 and you have a specific subdivision in which you would like to buy. Your agent can eliminate time and wasted mileage by punching a few buttons on his computer keyboard and printing out a list of the homes that meet your guidelines. He can further utilize his computer by requesting comparable sales opportunities in a given subdivision. It takes all of thirty or forty seconds to find out exactly what is available, as well as what is being sold.

Real estate agents know their city, and they know property values. As we have said before, it can be a valuable learning experience to spend a day with a real estate agent, driving around the city and discovering the areas you want to research.

The agent we work with is not involved in every deal. It is a mutually beneficial business relationship. She does not exert all her efforts in finding properties for us. We love to shop for our purchases ourselves. She tries to find us good properties for investment, and she does a great job because she knows that we are solid, qualified buyers and that we mean business. In the beginning we told many agents our needs, and many of them seemed interested. After leaving their offices, we expected our phones to be ringing off the wall. Unfortunately, they didn't. After a little experience, we found everyone was looking for the same kind of properties that we were.

One of our best buys was a little home in our target area that an agent called us about. We wrote an offer over the phone, "subject to our inspection of the property." The agent presented the offer fifteen minutes before another offer was brought in to the seller. If you know your area, be prepared to offer immediately. Often, only a quick and knowledgeable decision will make the difference between another lost deal and high profits.

On the other hand, real estate agents, like everyone else, are hoping to make money as a result of their time and effort. In most states a real estate agent charges from six to eight percent commission for services. This commission comes out of the price the buyer pays for the property. If you are investing in real estate to make your own profits, you must realize that this commission will probably cut into your profits. If you go through an agent to sell your homes all the time, you will be giving thousands of dollars to the agent who makes the sales. If you have structured your offer to take into account the commission that will be paid to a real estate agent, then by all means enlist the services of an agent. If not, you might be better off to think about it for a while before committing yourself. The services that an agent provides are certainly not impossible for you to do yourself.

With some knowledge and education you can look at properties without an agent. You can attend closings on purchases of properties without an agent. You can lease properties without an agent. You can put properties up for sale without an agent. You can show your properties yourself, without an agent. You must remember that these jobs all take a great deal of time. Perhaps if your realtor accomplishes some of these tasks for you, you will have time to buy even more properties and make even greater profits. You must decide what course will be the most profitable for you, but remember that you do have a choice.

When you are buying a home from a seller who is using a realtor, you will probably note that the agent does not include you in the presentation or the negotiation phases of the offer. In most cases, we have found that an agent prefers that you not talk directly with his client, but rather speak only through him. Realtors, whether they are working for the buyer or the seller, would rather be the only negotiators. We like to have a part in the transactions. We find that when we talk with the owner himself, we usually stand a better chance of understanding his needs and helping him understand ours. We are able to restructure our offers to meet his needs, and many times we walk away with a better price than our original offer.

Many realtors lack creativity. Many salesmen think it is a ridiculous myth that you can buy houses for a price far below the market value and then rent them in order to create a positive cash flow, or sell them at market value and make a hefty profit. These salesmen will tell you that such ideas were possible in the seventies, but those days are gone forever. We looked at a package of three duplexes and found that they weren't for us. We asked the realtor if he had any other properties to show us. He informed us that if we were looking for something with less then twenty percent down and a positive cash flow opportunity, we were looking for the impossible. As we had found and purchased many of these "impossible" properties, we knew that he was wrong. We thanked him and began looking for another agent, one who would understand our creative techniques and would be willing to present them.

When we first began investing, all three of us thought that all realtors were the same and that they would all do their utmost to help us find whatever we were looking for. This is not true. Some real estate people will try to negate your success, simply because they haven't seen what you are proposing accomplished and don't understand the techniques you are espousing. But all realtors are not narrow-minded; there are many creative realtors out there, and you will just have to find one. We found our agent through our local investment club.

If and when a good buy does appear, in the newspaper or in the MLS listing, it will not sit around for long. If an agent is aware of these wonderful purchases, he will realize that a great deal of work will be needed to find them. Keep in mind that real estate salesmen are usually aware of the advantages of investing, just as you are. If he puts a great deal of effort into finding great deals and actually does come up with a $75,000 home that is on the market for $52,000, an agent will probably purchase that property for himself. An agent is going to figure out in a hurry that *he* should buy that remarkably low-priced home. He will most likely end up by getting into real estate investing himself. An agent who is proficient at finding bargains may not work on your behalf for very long, not once he realizes what you're doing and how much money you're making from doing it.

Sometimes using a realtor can take longer than we like. Buying, rehabilitating, and selling a house takes long enough as it is—if we add a realtor to the process, it can add to the delay. He has to make an appraisal of the property, draw up a listing agreement, put the listing into MLS (it takes time for this to appear in the books), etc. Each day a house sits empty, waiting to be sold, costs us money. We prefer to speed up this process by doing our own advertising, showing, negotiating, and selling. This speeds up the time it takes for us to realize our profits. It did take us a while to become comfortable with the selling process, but now that we are, it definitely makes our ventures easier and faster.

In looking for an agent, ask your friends and relatives to recommend a good real estate agent, one they have worked with or heard about. You can also just pop into several agencies and discuss your needs as you assess the reactions of the agents and observe their responses.

Title Companies

A vital asset to your team is a title company. We use a title company to close all the deals that we make. For those who are unsure, a title company is a type of insurance company. The company will look up the title on any property and give you a detailed report on what liens and debts there are against the property for which a buyer would be liable. If a lien they did not find eventually shows up on a property, they will be responsible for paying that lien. We would not consider purchasing a home without a title company's report on it. We do know how to look up titles at the county courthouse, as we sometimes do to see if a property is worth pursuing. (We did it more often when we first began, since we did not want to pay for the title company's services if we found an obvious reason not to buy a house in that original search.) We always get a title company's guarantee along with our own discoveries. As this is their field of expertise, they are far better at finding hidden surprises than we are. Once the closing has occurred and the papers have been signed, you are locked in to a deal. Don't play Russian Roulette with your properties—use a title company.

A title company is not only an insurance company, it can help in many other ways as well. Our title officer has saved us thousands of dollars merely by answering questions. A good title officer can answer many of the questions you might at first go to an attorney for, and while he doesn't replace an attorney, he does charge a great deal less. The company will even help draw up contracts, if necessary. Also, title companies arrange our closings when we don't use a realtor—they supply all the papers and make certain that everything is in order. The closing is held in their office. All you need to do is show up with a cashier's check; the title company will let you know what the amount is in advance.

We call our title company several days prior to closing to find out the costs involved in the closing. If we are receiving a discount on the title insurance we're purchasing, then we'll find out the discount percentage. Because we try to use the same title company when we're able to choose, we receive a discount as sellers. As buyers, we always ask if the seller has a particular company in mind. If he does not, then we request our own "team member."

Where can you find a good title company? Your friendly realtor can make suggestions. If you have already dealt with a lawyer, ask him if he knows of a good title company (make sure you stress that you are not asking his *professional* opinion, for reasons to be explained below). Also ask any other investors you might know. The personal experience of others can lead to a title company you will be comfortable with. You'll learn through the closing process exactly how efficient a title company is, and then you can decide whether or not to deal with it again.

Using An Attorney

From time to time in your investment career you will need the advice of an attorney. We first used an attorney's time when we put together our partnership agreement. He can also draw up leases, contracts for sale (if you want to add to the ones you buy at the office supply shop), eviction notices, etc. You will also need a lawyer if one of the houses you've sold goes into foreclosure. Attorneys can be invaluable—an hour spent with an attorney can save you thousands of dollars. Do keep in mind, however, that attorneys are well aware of just how invaluable their advice is and have set their prices to represent that value. One hundred dollars an hour is not an unreasonable or unusual amount for an attorney to charge. Do not think that you can avoid those fees by giving him a quick call. He does not need to see your shining face to charge you for his time—he'll record the time when he begins speaking to you professionally and you'll receive an itemized bill later.

We learned this the hard way. Early on we went to an attorney and spent some time with him in his office. We then made several calls to him later, naively thinking the calls didn't count. When a $900 bill arrived we were alarmed and surprised, but we woefully paid the bill. Be aware now and your shock may not be as great.

You could avoid paying an attorney by reading up on law (a lengthy process, and where in the world would you start?) or going to law school yourself (an even more lengthy process, and after paying exorbitant law school fees, you would not have saved anything). If you have an attorney-relative who might give you some help for free, ask him or her your questions (but get this attorney to state what he will charge you for his services, even if it's your boyfriend, husband, or mother). If you're going to use an attorney you don't know, try to get a quote from him on the price for his service, not his per hour rate. Know your questions before you see your attorney, and do not spend much time over small talk while his professional timer is ticking.

Try to get a reference when looking for an attorney. An attorney who does a lot of real estate work will be very useful. Ask any other investors you know if they have used a good attorney. Your banker can tell you the lawyer he uses to process the bank's foreclosures. Again, shop prices. Ask your attorney his fee per hour or per case *before* you go in to speak with him. And keep it short! For an attorney, time is money. You may be able to get around that, though, if your title company has an in-house attorney available for you to consult.

Accountant

By the end of the first year in your investing career, you will probably need a good tax accountant if you have acquired several properties. You are not making just enough to get by anymore, and the government will undoubtedly want to share in your success. Look for an accountant who specializes in real estate and knows the latest real estate laws. Again, your realtor can send you in the right direction, as can your fellow investors.

Our accountant has taught us how to set up and keep our tax records. We meet with him quarterly to analyze our progress and discuss our possible tax benefits. You will not regret the fee you pay your accountant when you see how much he can save you in taxes.

Insurance Representative

When you purchase your first property, you will need a good insurance representative. You'll need insurance on all of your properties, and proof of paid insurance prior to the closing of your property. Ask your present insurance agent if he knows where you might find someone who can meet the insurance of your investment properties—he might be able to help you himself. Shop around. There are some companies that offer excellent rental-dwelling insurance plans.

Bankers

You should cultivate your business relationships with a few bankers. We think it's a good idea to know at least three of them by name at different banks. This way, you have three possibilities if you need a loan in a hurry. Once the bankers know you and what a dependable customer you are, they will be happy to see you every time you enter the bank.

Each time you make a trip to the bank, make it a point to go inside and deal face-to-face with the bank personnel. Use the Drive-Thru windows as little as possible. Get to know the tellers by name, as well as the people who staff the customer service department. Some day you may need a friend!

We would like to add how important your appearance is when you're meeting with any of your team members. You are a businesswoman now, and you should dress like one whenever you deal with other businessmen or professionals, such as your real estate agent, your lawyer, your title company representatives, your accountant, and your insurance agent. They will all treat you more seriously if you dress for success. Every time you go into the bank, try to look your best. Imagine you are wearing a nice suit or dress, and you're going to make a money transaction. Smile and try to catch the attention of your friendly banker—the one who loans you so much money. You're in a hurry to make even more money, and he's busy also, but take a moment or two to walk over and say hello if he isn't on the phone or with another customer. This will make a difference. If you have been working on a rehab project all day at one of your properties and are in your grubby clothes, it might be a good idea to skip a trip to the bank that day.

Repairmen

As the number of your properties increases, you will begin to need a good plumber and a reliable electrician. We do not choose to deal with tough plumbing projects or with involved electrical problems. These are intricate and dangerous fields that we all agreed early on would not be easy to learn from a do-it-yourself book. You will need a handyman who can take care of assorted tasks, from trimming the bushes to hauling the trash. You can find such workers by looking through the want ads in the local paper, checking out the bulletin boards at restaurants and grocery stores, or by asking some of your more reliable acquaintances. Or you could even place an ad in the paper, advertising your needs.

Although we started out doing our own repair work and redecorating, we are now finding we can add to our successes by using more of our brains and less of our backs. You will need these repairmen as time goes by, even though you do not need to have one in mind before making your first offer on your first house.

Merchants

It is also a good idea to start looking around for some stores at which you can open accounts. You will be buying large amounts of wallpaper, paint, carpet, and hardware—see if you can open an account at each of the different stores that provide these products. If you have an account, you can simply charge your purchases and not have to worry about having cash with you every time you enter the store. It is also much easier to keep records of your expenses when you receive an itemized bill once a month. You may even be able to negotiate a discount because you buy so much and so often. Keep your eyes open for a good copy shop—you are going to make copies of many of your official documents, and unless you have your own copier, you're going to need a place to have this done. You might be able to open an account there too.

Let's review the people you'll need to add to your team: 1) A real estate agent who is aware of creative, interesting techniques; 2) an efficient title company; 3) an attorney and an accountant who specialize in real estate and investment laws; 4) a good insurance representative; 5) at least three bankers; 6) dependable repairmen for those problems that are beyond your abilities; 7) stores that allow charges and give discounts for bulk purchasing; 8) a good copy shop.

All of the people you have added to your team will be indispensable. But do not lie awake at night worrying about where you'll find them and what they will cost. All of this will come in time. Keep your eyes open for some potentially reliable team members, and keep looking for interesting properties. The players on your team will come along as you need them.

CHAPTER SIX

Let's Go
Shopping!

PICTURE THE LADY, you know the one: She plans weeks ahead
of time to attend the annual lingerie sale at her favorite department store.
Then she grabs the girdles and pulls them from those weaker than she.
Shopping is something we women are good at.

All right, ladies, we've talked about it long enough. Let's go shopping for
real and buy your first investment.

We look for many things when we look for a home. The most important,
of course, is price range. We must make a profit, obviously, or this would not
be a profitable career. We ascertain before we go shopping how much we can
spend on a home, and from there we know what to look for. We look for homes
priced below market, and usually end up doing some work on these houses
to get them ready to rent or sell, though not all of our houses have required
work. We use various types of financing (to be explained at length in the financing chapter), and the financing method we plan to use on any given investment determines how we will structure our offer. Once we're owners, we do any
necessary rehabilitation, and then we put our property on the market. We then
start taking in a positive cash flow, or refinance for some cash to buy another
home.

Easy enough, right? Let's go into each one of our steps, keeping in mind
the woman buying her first investment home. You'll be nervous, but don't worry—
eventually this will become as natural as a trip to the grocery store. You'll know

what to look for without looking it up in a book and you'll trust your own judgment.

We want to remind you before you begin to monitor your attitude: Go shopping with positive expectations—you are going to buy a property. Do not think of the million and one reasons you should wait until next year to buy. Bargains are not on the market for long—they quickly become closed deals. So let's go! Let's get this scary first home bought.

Price

First, you need to establish the amount of money you plan to spend on your home. Remember, this does not necessarily have to be your own money. (See our chapter on financing, for ideas on where to get money.) You need to establish the amount of money you can spend: your price range. When looking at any home, remember to keep some money aside for fix-up. Don't put every penny you have into the down payment so that you have no money left to buy a gallon of paint.

You need to have in mind how much you intend to offer as a down payment. You need to know what kind of payments the house can support per month and the time frame for rehabilitation. A very important consideration at this point is whether you plan to lease option, sell, rent, or refinance your property. If you plan to sell it, or refinance, you must get all cash invested back out of it. Whatever you do with your property, it must be done quickly. Every day you own that home with no tenant or new buyer is costing you money. This means your fix-up must be finished as quickly as possible, not when you get around to it. We keep this in mind and set the closing date for a time that the needed repairs will take. Then we work very hard to get that house ready to rent or sell as soon as possible.

Every purchase should be profitable in some respect. If there are excessive rentals in a particular area at a particular time, you may have a difficult time renting your property. This is why it is so important to know your area. Call about ads for rentals, and drive around the neighborhood. Are there many "For-Rent" signs scattered through the neighborhood? What are owners charging for rents in a certain area? (There is a difference between what owners are making and what they are asking.) Notice how many houses are for sale: Are they selling? For how much? We cannot stress how important this information can be. You will have to make many calls, but this is part of the process that will lead to a larger paycheck with fewer mistakes.

We realize you probably don't have much money to spend on this first deal—we didn't have much money on our first deals either. This is why you are looking for a very special deal on your first buy. It will take you longer to find, partly because it will be a fantastic deal that does not come along too often, partly because of how cautious and nervous you are. It took us three months after reading our first books on real estate investing to buy our first properties. We studied all possible options and did a lot of shopping. Do not worry about this first delayed buy—Rome was not built in a day, and your career will take some time before it's a sturdy structure. We looked at many, many properties before we made our first offer.

We like to buy small, single-family homes in the lower price range; in our area that means under $70,000. This is certainly not the only way to go, but that is usually what we look for. It might be your best bet as a first buy.

Let's make the first one the easiest of all—an owner-financed buy. (These are easiest to find when interest rates are high.) The seller of this home has given up on the regular process of selling; interest rates are so high that most buyers have become discouraged. But the seller still needs to sell his home. Perhaps he's been transferred, maybe there's been a death or a divorce and the house has become a burden. Whatever the reason, the current owner is offering to "loan" you the money to buy this home. You will see such homes advertised in the papers as "owner financed"—circle all of these homes in your area and get on the phone.

Owner-financed homes are a great way to get started. If your credit rating is not strong enough yet, a home owner will be more flexible than a regular lender would be, and there will be many possibilities open to you. You can lease the home and allow your tenant to help you make your monthly payments. A year or so later, when your credit rating has more punch to it, perhaps interest rates will drop so you can refinance this home. Why should you want to refinance a home? Because you have bought this home under its market value. The bank or loan institution, however, does not look at what you actually paid for a property; it is concerned with what the house is worth right now. The bank will get an appraisal and will usually finance about eighty percent of the appraised value. You can take this cash from your new loan and pay off the owner from whom you "borrowed" money to buy the home. Whatever you have left over is yours to keep—and remember, any money you have left over is borrowed money and therefore *tax free* until you sell.

Shall we talk numbers? Suppose you come upon a house that appears to be in deplorable condition but actually just needs to be thoroughly cleaned inside and out—maybe it also needs a coat of paint. Your intuition tells you that it is a good deal and you're certain you can fix it up to rent quickly. The owner knows that this house is a mess; he's had it on the market for four months and people are just not interested. He's really desperate because he and his wife have split up and he needs the money out of the house as soon as possible. You make an offer of $40,000 with five percent down—$2,000. You ask for a thirty-year loan at ten percent interest, which makes your payment (with taxes and insurance) about $400 per month. You become the owner of this home and fix it up. As it is a three-bedroom, you are able to rent it out for $550 per month (you now have a positive cash flow of $150 per month). A year goes by— you've been making your payments right on time and your rental is still bringing in that extra cash. Because you have worked so hard on your credit rating, it smells like a rose and bankers smile when they see you. You refinance this home. What a pleasant surprise! The home you bought for $40,000 has been appraised by the bank for $58,000! They will give you eighty percent of this amount, so you receive a check for $46,400. With this money, you pay off the owner what you owe him ($40,000 minus your $2,000 and twelve payments on the principal—which equals about $37,800). You now have $8,000. Once you take out $2,000 for your original investment, you have $6,000 in tax free profit! You can go out to lunch, or better yet, go out and do the same thing with three more houses. This isn't a bad career, is it?

So you are looking for homes advertised in the paper or around town as "owner financed." Another thing that you want to be on the lookout for is an ad that claims "owner desperate." Give this person a call. Is there any mention of "flexible terms"? This could include a seller who is willing to carry some or all of the financing, or a seller who wants strictly cash but will negotiate on the price. Fifteen percent of the houses that you will find in the paper are offering flexible terms—find them! Do not wait to find all the perfect terms listed in one ad; you will probably never get out of your house if you do. If you ever do come across an ad that says, "Nothing down, owner financing, underpriced, seller desperate," you can rest assured that seller is very busy answering his phone. Go ahead and call, but don't get your hopes up too high. You probably couldn't dial fast enough to talk to that owner—somebody else will probably have already bought the house before you ever get an answer to your call.

We've found that Monday is the best day of the week for making ad calls. Sellers often place their ads in the paper so they will run for eight days, beginning on Sunday. If you happen to call on the first Monday, after the non-business Sunday, you stand a good chance of having first pick. If the second Monday rolls around and the ad is still there, you'll find at the other end of the phone line an owner who is beginning to get very discouraged. Help him out. You'll also find that it is easier and faster to read through Monday's ads than Sunday's. On Sunday, every real estate agency in town is advertising the homes they have listed. Many of these will not be of interest to you, so it might be in your best interest to pay more attention to what Monday has to offer if you are looking for a home for sale by owner.

Questions to Ask on the Phone

We have drawn up a list of questions you should ask the owner when making your calls. The questions on the price and the terms are the most important. If the answers you receive to these questions do not show promise, then there is no reason to waste your time by going out to see the house.

What is the price (if this information is not listed in the advertisement)? The answer to this question could cause you to end the conversation very quickly. The seller may say something like, "We are asking . . . " This answer already indicates flexibility. If the seller is willing to negotiate over the price, you may have something to discuss, even if the starting figure is a little too high for you. And you might not even need his flexibility if you are informed enough about the area to know whether his asking price is reasonably below the market value of the home. We once paid the full asking price for a home that we knew was priced $10,000 below its market value.

Get a good description of the home. Find out if there is a basement, a fireplace, or a double garage. If you have done your research on the neighborhood and the current appraisal values, you will be able to know whether his price is too high, just about average, or too low.

What is the address? Be sure the house is in a safe neighborhood, a neighborhood in which you feel good about working. Look for a neighborhood that would meet your own needs; find a neighborhood you would like to move into yourself. Is property in this area appreciating? Will you be able to rent this house quickly to good tenants and establish a cash flow?

Why are you selling? *This is very important.* You can find out how motivated the seller is to find a buyer. You will also have a hint of what his needs are and whether you can meet them. You may also learn that you do not want to be the owner of the house. If there have been six cases of arson on the block in the last month, or he is moving because his house has been broken into and vandalized several times in the past year, you might be better off looking elsewhere. Is the house vacant? A vacant home is costing someone money, and probably indicates a very motivated seller. Vacant homes do not look quite as good to the average buyer as an occupied home. The seller may be very ready to accept any offer.

What are the terms? Is there an assumable loan? Will the owner finance? If he answers "Yes" to one of the latter two questions, and the price is flexible or under-market, you can let yourself feel a little bit of excitement.

If the loan is assumable, what is the balance due on the loan? In other words, how much equity is in the house? This is important because you must know how much money you will need in order to meet the asking price, in the form of a second mortgage or cash. The owner might be willing to carry his equity in the form of a second mortgage.

What is the monthly payment on the first mortgage? Does that include taxes and insurance? What are those charges, if not? If you are hoping to assume this loan, you must know if you will be able to handle the payment.

What is the percentage rate on the first mortgage? Is the first mortgage assumable at this percentage rate? Is it a non-qualifying loan, FHA, VA? If so, life will be much simpler for you!

How many years before the first loan will be paid off? If there are only a few years left before the loan will be completely paid, you will have to come up with a bigger second mortgage. If that is the case, you might want to structure your offer differently.

Are there any other mortgages? If so, is the second mortgage assumable? If there is a first mortgage that has a $14,000 balance at nine percent interest, the house may seem inviting to you. But if there is a second mortgage with a balance of $20,000 that is not assumable, or that is at a high interest rate, you must first pay off that second mortgage. This means qualifying for a conventional loan in most cases, or taking out a second mortgage of your own through a bank.

What is the zoning? A realtor would know this; an owner might not. If you are planning to use this property as a rental, you need to make a call and ask about the zoning before going further with your interest in this property. Look up the proper number in the telephone book under "county governments." Get the zoning report in writing from your county. Commercial zoning may mean higher rents.

These questions about the house itself are also important:
How old is the house; the roof; the furnace?
What is the square footage?
How many bedrooms? Size?
How many bathrooms?
Is there a garage? One car or two car?
Is there a basement? Finished or unfinished? How big?
Is there a family room? Fireplace?
Are there any appliances?

Do you get the idea of the kind of questions you are asking? A couple of optional questions might be: What condition is the house in? Does it need much work? How big is the lot? Is there a patio? Is the yard fenced?

Needs

On each house you buy you should have a goal for that property to be accomplished by a certain time. This will help you determine your price range and the terms you need. And what are your money needs? Your needs are constantly changing, so know what you need from a property. Do you want to rent this home to tenants or sell it again quickly? Are you looking for immediate profits or tax benefits and appreciation?

Ask the owner what his needs are. If, for instance, he is trying to buy another house, he probably needs all of his money in a hurry so that he can get into that house—he needs his equity immediately. If immediate cash is not necessary, he might be willing to carry a loan. Ascertain what you are each looking for and try to come to a compromise. If you can somehow make the two needs match up, you may have the basis for a deal beneficial to both of you.

If you are finding it difficult to buy a house right now due to a lack of money—you can't even make a down payment—you may want to consider another alternative. You could lease a home with an option to buy. A lease option gives a renter the option to buy the house he is presently renting from the owner— he may buy this house on or before the date agreed upon by both of them. While the renter is making these payments, a certain amount is going toward the down payment of the house.

This is a good way to go if you are lacking funds, because it eliminates the need for a full down payment at a time when you may not have it. (You do have to pay an option deposit, however, so you need a relatively small amount of cash. On a lease option, you will sometimes get this deposit back if you do not buy the home.) This way you can get into a home and yet not have a full commitment to buy it. Make sure that you have the right to sublet the property to a tenant who can make your payments for you.

If you are planning to invest a great deal of money, energy, and time into this home you have leased with an option, then make sure you have a binding and legal contract or lease. Often these options can be recorded with the court-house in the county.

Now you're ready to look at the homes you have made calls about and you're interested in. Remember to take your mortgage payment table with you. This makes it easier to figure what type payments you will be making on any property. If you don't have an amortization schedule yet, take your financial calculator with you.

We have found that a good time to shop is when the sky clouds over and snow or rain begins to fall. On dismal days, owners often become discouraged and are very happy to see you. Perhaps the sellers are having visions of Phoenix or Miami as the snow falls. While they're considering how cold their toes are, is an excellent time to discuss terms with them. You should be ready to go shop-ping if you read an article in the paper that says that real estate values are down and houses simply are not moving. This makes owners nervous, and they are even happier to see you. But don't take the papers too seriously. Any temporary lull in the market is just that—temporary. While it is in a lull, some great deals will be made. Don't get left behind.

Shopping for Values

Once you are out looking, whatever the weather, be aware of how many homes are for sale on a single block and know their values. Then talk to the owner of the property that interests you. Try to buy the worst house on the block instead of the best. If there is only one bad house on the block, it may be nothing but a bad apple that needs to be renovated into a good one again. But if a well-kept house is surrounded by homes that are not looked after, it could well be a sign that the neighborhood is losing ground. You want to be careful of the neighborhood in which you buy. As you advance in real estate investing, you may be able to change the fate of a neighborhood by buying up a whole block of these homes and fixing them up. But avoid this strategy on your first buy.

Remember that all money makers are not fix-ups. It makes sense, doesn't it, that there will be more foreclosures with the interest rate at thirteen percent instead of eight percent? People get into more trouble with their payments at these higher interest rates. Their house may be in perfect repair, but they need to sell in a hurry. They need some cash. They quickly put their house up for sale and put an ad in the paper. If you make enough calls and drive around enough, you're going to find many situations like this. It takes work and it takes time, but they're out there. We have found them, and so can you.

When you go house hunting, take a note pad with you. As you go through a property, write down everything you observe. You will need to review these notes to find out what needs to be done in order to either rent the house or sell it for profit. This will give you an idea of fix-up costs. Ask the owner questions about the house: Has he been happy with it? Has he had any problems with it? Does he like the neighborhood? His answers will reveal much.

Location

Always consider the location of a prospective buy. Is there an auto garage across the street? Is there a noisy highway just behind the property that makes it difficult to hear what the owner is saying? Such houses are more difficult to rent and sell. And remember that the area must be a safe one. If you are going to show that property after dark, you don't want to be constantly looking over your shoulder.

Structure

How well is the house built? Be sure it is structurally sound. If there is a basement, is it likely to be made of poured concrete? Go down there and take a look around. Do the foundations look sturdy? Put your back against a wall and look down the wall you are standing against. Is the wall bending or buckling? If not, the foundation is probably a solid one. If you do notice some buckling, you are better off moving on, because that house probably needs major work (about $5,000 per wall) and you will be responsible for the repairs if you become the owner. A few cracks may be okay, but a faulty foundation is not. If you question the foundation or the roof, or some other major aspect of repair, then you may make your offer contingent upon inspection by an expert on foundations, roofs, furnaces, or anything else you are concerned about. Write this into your contract or purchase offer.

If the house is sitting on a concrete block basement and there are foundation problems, they will be easier and less expensive to fix, but you will still have a substantial amount in repair costs. If there is a crawl space, take a look at it. We always like to take along flashlights with us to check out dark corners like this that could be hiding trouble spots. How does it look? Is it dry? Is there a problem with flooding on a regular basis? Ask the owner; you need to be cautious. If water has seeped in because of a particularly violent rainstorm recently, this water can be pumped out and a pump could be installed, but the cost for having this done must be added into your overall assessment of the house.

Use your trusty flashlight to check the insulation in the attic. If there is no insulation, once again, this should be included in any repair estimate.

If you are in a part of the country that has problems with termites, take a pocket knife with you so that you can test the home for infestation. Take the knife and stab it into one of the rafters in the garage, attic, basement, or laundry room. We did this when we first went home shopping without quite knowing the reason we were doing it. So that you are not left as confused as we were, what you are checking is whether the wood feels solid or unsturdy. You want to see if the structure will be around for another forty years. If it does not feel dependable—if it gives easily—then that home may have some unseen tenants who are one day going to make their presence known. Termite problems are something you will need to address in the contract. The owners will usually be responsible for a reasonable amount of repair. How does the roof look? If the building has a flat roof, is there any evidence of water damage on the ceilings inside? We have bought homes that needed new roofs, but that additional cost must be added on.

How do the floors look? Have they settled or sagged in places? Be wary of this—even a great decorator will have a difficult time covering this up.

Plumbing and Electrical

Turn on the water (if the water is on) and flush a toilet. Does there seem to be a plumbing problem? Check the faucets, tubs, and showers. Turn off the water for the entire house (ask the owner to do this for you) and take a look to see if the meter is still going. If it is, there may be a leak in the main line and you want to be careful.

Mechanical Inspection

If you are seriously considering buying this house, you will need to have a mechanical inspection done to make certain that everything is working well. You make the arrangements and pay for this inspection. Ask your realtor to help you find a good inspector. (When you have this done, tag along with the inspector. Learn what it is he looks for, and ask questions. That way you know what to look for in the future.) Always make certain that the owner is on the premises when the mechanical inspection is performed. Otherwise, your inspector may miss a broken water line and you'll buy that house unaware of what could be a thousand-dollar expense. This happened to us once—we hope you can avoid it.

If the house is structurally sound, and the owner seems ready to negotiate, start talking to him. You may be on the trail of your first buy.

Looking Beyond Imperfection

Do not be afraid of a house that looks rather odd at first glance. Take another look: Is the basic floor plan really that bad, or does it look odd due to some handyman's additions? We once bought a home that looked very different and unattractive because of what some ingenious fellow had done to it. Perhaps he liked it, but the house had not sold because of his additions in the garage and basement. We saw that this was repairable and made an offer on the home. Because the property had been on the market for so long, we paid a bargain price for it. We had a handyman tear out all of the former owner's additions and the house looked normal again. It proved a very good buy.

As long as a house has two or three bedrooms, is structurally sound, and has a reasonable price, that purchase is probably not going to be a mistake, as long as you can rent it and cover your monthly obligations. If you can swing the financing and buy the house at a reduced price, go ahead and talk to the owner. Do not put too much thought into whether you would buy this particular house to live in yourself. Consider instead whether someone else would either rent it or buy it from you.

Falling in Love—Don't Do It

As long as we're talking about the attitude you need to have when looking for a property, we would like to add that it is not good business to fall in love with one of your investment properties. We had problems with this at first. We saw so much potential in homes—there was just so much that we could do to

88

make them into real treasures. We had to deal with this when we were rehabbing the property with the ingenious former owner. Our first impulse was: "Let's fix it up really nice! We can show him how it should have been done!" When we considered the cost of doing this, however, we realized it was not a good idea. You will eventually come to care for this home so much that you will not be able to part with it or even rent it. Approach any purchase as an investment, not as your own home. Decide to put a certain amount into rehabilitation and when you have spent that amount, stop with your rehab.

It is easy for women to get carried away with projects. Yes, it would be a wonderful world if all the houses in it could look as nice as yours, but you do not need to pay for the earth's entire housing renovation. Before you spend money for any part of rehabilitation, decide if it will bring in more rent or sell for more due to this expenditure. You should make the house clean and comfortable and leave it to someone else to make it a showcase.

You must remember that buying homes is not your hobby; it is your career, the way you make enough money to put bread on the table. Your bottom-line consideration is dollars and cents. This might sound harsh, but force yourself to be realistic—this is a business. The money you spend on rehabilitation must be worth the expense. If it isn't, then you are spending your profits.

Some Hints on Great Buys

There are probably some areas in your town that are perfect for your investments. We have been especially lucky with old FHA and VA loans. Some areas of town have many houses that were originally bought with these loans, and they are profitable because of their underlying loans. If you can assume these loans and find a home that is priced below market, you could have the ingredients for a classic cash-flow property. If there is an army base in your town, keep your eyes open for any house near it that is for sale. If that house has an old VA loan on it that is assumable, this is definitely a point in its favor. To assume FHA and VA loans, there is only a forty-five dollar transfer fee and you are the owner of a home without the normal qualifying hassles.

You may want to look at the lists put out by the Federal Housing Administration and the Veterans Administration of houses that have been taken back because the owner was not making payments. Most real estate agents will have access to these lists—ask for one. These homes are usually reasonably priced. You can often purchase with little and get government financing, but you must qualify.

Check out areas that are being developed. If an area is going to be getting

89

some new facilities built, you want to study the potential increase in value the neighborhood could experience. Read your local papers and know what is being planned. Try to purchase some below-market properties in these areas. In our community, we bought some properties in an area with a new highway being developed nearby. These houses were bargain-priced in the first place—we had a positive cash flow coming in on them from the beginning. We now are watching their value go up as the months go by. Many businesses are interested in moving onto the new four-lane highway, and they will have to buy our home to do so. We expect to eventually do very well with this property.

We purchased another property on a double lot within a few feet of a new four-lane street. Our property is in the process of being changed to commercial zoning and will be worth about five times the price we paid for it.

A successful technique we have used in looking for homes is to simply drive around an area. We pinpoint an area that looks interesting to us and then two of us go out to learn what we can about it. While one drives, the other takes down the address of any house that is either for sale or appears to be in distress. Perhaps a house has overgrown grass and weeds all over the front yard, or it looks vacant or forlorn. That house needs us, and since it has fallen into disrepair, the owner just might be willing to talk to us, even if the property is not for sale. And he might be willing to sell it for a bargain price.

Take the addresses you have scribbled down and give your courthouse a call. Ask to speak with the clerk in the records department and inquire who the owners of these properties are. Once you have the name, you can find the owner and see if he is interested in selling. We did this once and found that four of the houses we had on our list were actually for sale, or were being considered for sale, but the signs weren't up. You just never know what you might find.

One day as we were driving, we spotted a new "For Sale By Owner" sign. The property looked like one we would like to own, so we wrote down the pertinent information. The sign said to call after four but we got restless and started calling at three. We reached the owner and he told us the price of the house. We were shocked. We felt his price was $10,000 below the fair market value. He was offering owner financing with a low down payment, and the interest rate was only ten percent! This sounded too good to be true—we hadn't even negotiated! We arranged to meet in fifteen minutes. We went through the house and we were very pleased with it—it was exactly the type of house we were looking for. How long do you think we delayed in making an offer? We gave him an earnest deposit on the spot and by four we had a contract. As we were leaving, another prospective buyer pulled up to buy the house. He had just missed a very good deal. The moral of the story: move quickly on a bargain. Make your offer, and sign a contract.

Foreclosures

Many investors like to go after properties that are in foreclosure. You will find that this could be a very profitable way for you to go. Houses that have gone into foreclosure are eventually auctioned off to the general public if the bills on those houses are not paid. Usually, the house is auctioned for the amount of the loan against it. Many of these homes are not bought at the auction and end up going back to the bank that financed the loan. The former owner of the house is given a grace period in which he can pay off what he owes and redeem his house. This is called a redemption period—the length of this redemption period varies from state to state. If the owner does not redeem the house within that period, he loses all rights to it and the bank is free to sell the house.

Lending organizations do not like these foreclosed homes one bit. They call these properties R.E.O.'s (Real Estate Owned). They are money lenders, not real estate agencies or investors. They want to get such properties off their books as soon as possible. We do not usually pick up houses at a public trustee sale (where houses in foreclosure are auctioned off) because in our state, the redemption period is six months. This is too long to have our cash tied up. Instead, we contact lending agencies and ask if they have any houses that have been taken back that they're trying to sell. This is one method that has brought us some marvelous buys.

If you are interested in foreclosures, we recommend several books about buying property in distress. You would enjoy Wade Cook's book on foreclosures. You will need to study the laws of your state and then decide whether this area is worth your while to pursue.

Multi-family Units

We have talked about buying single-family homes almost exclusively. But what if you come up on a multi-family unit that looks very good to you?

Do not be afraid if it is your first buy. Remember, our first purchase was two five-plexes and one four-plex, and we survived the trauma. In fact, we are very proud of that first buy.

There is one definite advantage in buying any sort of a multi-family unit. If one unit is vacated, you are not left with a totally empty building on which you're making the entire payment. The other units are still rented and helping you meet your monthly mortgage payments.

The main disadvantage in buying apartment complexes is that they require more management. Before you purchase one, make certain that you know what you are going to do with it once it's yours.

You need to determine a gross scheduled income if you come across a complex you would like to buy. To do this, either get a pencil and paper or get out your calculator. Due to your research, you have already ascertained what your building will provide in the way of rent. Multiply all the rents you should receive in a month by twelve (twelve months in a year). You have just calculated your gross scheduled income (GSI). Now, we are going to guess that throughout the year you will have a five percent vacancy rate; so, take that first number—your GSI—and multiply it by .05. Subtract this number from the GSI to see what you can make in a single year from your properties.

You aren't finished. Now that you have an idea what your income is for a single year with your multi-family unit, you must plan for all those assorted fees you will pay as a landlord. These are management fees, insurance, taxes, supplies, trash fees, landscaping, pool service (if there is one), maintenance, snow removal, etc. Subtract all these fees from what you expect to take in from your building and see if it is still worth it. Can you make your payments? Do you have a positive cash flow? We considered all this and decided that buying a multi-family complex was worth the money. You may decide that sticking to single-family homes is a better idea. It is your decision.

You are probably still hesitant about buying your first investment property. But face it: you are never going to feel completely prepared to buy, so don't wait forever. Try to look at homes with reasons to buy instead of reasons not to buy. What is most important is good structure, a pleasing floor plan, a good location, and favorable financing. If you have these four items in a house you are thinking of buying, you probably have found a bargain. If you look hard enough for a reason not to buy a house, you will undoubtedly find it. There will always be some reason not to buy a home—a leaky faucet, peeling paint, or an ugly interior. Do not concentrate on these negatives—they are so easily corrected that they should not stay that way. If everything major looks appealing and your intuition is giving you a green light, do not sit around waiting—make an offer. To overcome fear you must act on what you are afraid of—actions conquer fear.

CHAPTER SEVEN

Making
Your Offer

I T'S TWO A.M.; your eyes are open wide. The only light in the room
is from the clock on the nightstand, and the only sound is the quiet click
as the numbers fall into place once a minute. But sleep is hopeless now,
since your head is filled with numbers and your stomach with butterflies. Today you meet the seller face to face and make your first offer!

We lived for months on adrenaline in place of sleep; our nights were filled
with excited planning. Once we understood the basics of negotiating and making
offers, it became an addicting game to lay awake and plan, exciting offers keeping us awake night after night. In this chapter we will help you capitalize on
those great ideas and actually present your first offer.

We'll start off with the assumption that you have found a property that looks
interesting. You've called about a classified ad, or perhaps have found the owner
of a deserted house. In any case, you think you have a good deal lined up and
you're ready to talk to the owner. What, where, and how will you talk to him,
her, or them?

Call the seller and make an appointment to meet face to face. You should
have at least driven by the property, and you are aware of its general condition—
from the outside. If it is a total wreck and you think the seller would be embarrassed by its condition, by all means make an appointment to meet on the
premises; not to embarrass the owner, but because your offer will be accepted
more readily if you make it as you look around the room with some degree
of apprehension, shaking your head and muttering, "At least a gallon of 409 . . . "

One time Jane called and told us to get on our grubbies, since we were going to the worst property we had ever seen. We let ourselves in through the missing windows, frightening cockroaches and termites who considered this their home. The condition was deplorable and the odor matched. We embarrassed the lender who had foreclosed on this duplex property by inviting him to meet us at the property. When we checked the plumbing under the sink we discovered it was missing altogether! It seemed he would be willing to accept a very low offer. We bought this property, which will always be known as our "yucky" duplex. The lender accepted our offer of $29,000 and loaned us an additional $10,000 for fix-up expenses. He was anxious to unload the deplorable mess! It certainly helped us establish our "track record" with that banker. We have used the same bank many times since.

If, however, the house is within the realm of normalcy, agree to meet somewhere else: don't give the owner the home-field advantage. Find a neutral meeting place, such as a local diner, or the park. Both parties will feel more comfortable.

If you're feeling nervous about the meeting, use the old trick of picturing the owner in nothing but an old pair of polka-dot shorts. It does work! Remember, he is just a person. It's been interesting for us to find that women seem to have a natural advantage when dealing with men. They trust us more, and they are less likely to feel they can take advantage of us. Old sex roles may not always be fair, but there are times when they are advantageous to us, and this is one of those times.

If there is a realtor involved, try to meet with the seller anyway. The realtor won't like it, but you will always get a better deal when talking to the seller on a personal level.

Before you can present any offer to a seller you must consider two things carefully. The first of these is your own goal for the property: The house must be able to support itself. The second thing to consider is the seller's needs. This is where your womanly talents and skills come in. You're basically using those same techniques you used when Dad wanted to eat oysters on the half shell and the kids wanted burgers and fries. Try to read each other's minds, anticipate responses, and be prepared to soothe the ruffled spots. Gather any information you can about the seller via the realtor or over the phone before you structure any offer.

Let us cite an example of how this technique has worked for us. Not too long ago a realtor who knew our business called us to say she had a package of two small houses located side by side on a well-traveled street in the nicest area in our city. The sellers, we found after questioning our realtor, were an elderly couple who had owned the houses for approximately fifty years. As a matter of fact, the couple had been married in one of the homes and had built the other as a rental unit. Later in life they'd moved and both pieces of property had become rentals. The couple were sentimentally attached to these properties but their children did not want the homes in their current state of disrepair (a result of destructive tenants).

The asking price was already unbelievably low at $49,950 for the two homes. Through further questioning we discovered that a young couple had contracted to buy both homes for $46,000 and had gone through the process of applying with a mortgage lender. The poor elderly couple had been hassled with mechanical inspections and termite inspections, and appraisers had left them with a lengthy list of needed repairs, and there had been closing costs to pay. On top of that, after several weeks the young buyers were turned down and the elderly couple had their property back.

This is where we came into the picture. Knowing the history of the couple and their property, we structured our own offer. We offered $37,500 cash. We asked for no appraisal, no termite or mechanical inspections; we would pay all closing costs including title insurance, and close in two weeks. This was a totally hassle-free offer to the couple, who signed it that evening without even making a counter offer.

At this point, you're thinking to yourself, I don't have $37,500 cash to offer on a piece of property! Neither did we. We borrowed $34,000 cash from our bank at the current rate (quite high), and an additional $6,000 to fix up the property. There was no problem with this, since the property had been appraised much higher than this anyway.

If you work very hard on a track record with a bank—by this we mean pay bills on time, keep a scrapbook, and keep them up to date on your business— you'll be able to make offers like this as well.

Two weeks later we owned these homes. We had them rehabilitated and leased for $395 and $350. Then we applied to refinance the properties to put on long-term mortgages and pull out some of our tax free profit!

When you make an offer, start at a price lower than what you actually hope to pay. In Roger Dawson's excellent book on negotiating, *You Can Get Anything You Want, But You Have to Do More than Ask*, he suggests that you decide exactly what your negotiating range is before you begin the negotiation. That is, figure out the highest price you're willing to pay, the price you feel you'll actually pay, and the price you will begin your offer with. For example, you may feel the house is worth $70,000, and you're willing to pay as much as $68,000.

Now you have established the top of your negotiating range. What price do you actually think you'll pay? Perhaps it's $65,000. Fine; now, how much should you start your offer with? How about $60,000? You have established your negotiating range, and you're ready to negotiate.

When you make your opening offer ($60,000, in the example), watch the seller carefully, and *be still*. Since you know the house is actually worth about $70,000, there is a strong tendency to make the $60,000 offer and then apologize, or excuse yourself for making such a low offer. Resist the impulse and put the burden on the seller.

When your seller begins to speak, listen to what he says. If his price is firm, perhaps he's willing to adjust his terms and you can increase your cash flow—see if he is willing to lower the interest rate. Just use your head, remain calm, and remember that you're negotiating from a point of strength. He probably has only one house to sell, but there are thousands of houses for you to buy. You have all the cards in your hand because you have far more options than he does.

Do not be afraid to ask for what you want from an owner. This is a difficult thing to learn. Women are accustomed to asking about and meeting another's needs. We have been raised to try to make everybody happy at once and not consider ourselves. Compromise is necessary in this business, but you must keep your profit in mind and strive to keep it a healthy, successful business. Just as you ask what the seller's needs are, you must be willing to state yours. If you don't ask, you'll never know if he would have been agreeable.

We once were dealing with a savings and loan that had taken back a house due to a foreclosure. Their advertised price for the home was $45,000. We knew it couldn't hurt to ask, so we offered $29,000 for the property. As long as we were being audacious, we figured we might as well go the full distance and ask for an additional $10,000 to fix up the property and to pay ourselves for doing it. All of this we wanted at an interest rate of ten percent with no payments until the work was completed. The going interest rate was three and one half points higher than that, so you can see that we were asking for quite a bit. But the savings and loan gave us what we asked for. Later, we asked ourselves just how much better a deal could have been made if we'd known how flexible they would be. So always ask, even though it seems outrageous to you. The deal you offer may be exactly what a seller is looking for, or he may be so desperate that he'll take anything.

Make your offer coincide with your goal for the property. If you plan to resell the property, you need to buy the home for a lower price or on terms that allow you to wrap a loan (see wraparounds in the next chapter). A house bought at a lower price will give you an instant return and profit on your money.

If you're planning to rent the property, your biggest concerns are the down payment and monthly mortgage payment. These must be low enough for you to get a renter into your property and have him make your mortgage payments for you. We don't believe in buying a negative cash flow. If you also feel this is a good policy to adopt, walk away from negotiations that are not going to provide you with an answer to this need.

As you are negotiating with a seller you may want to remind him of how much less he'll pay in income taxes if you pay for his house over a period of years rather than in one lump sum. Uncle Sam will take a considerable part of any large amount of cash that comes in a lump sum. If he needs the cash (he's buying another home, for instance), this will not be very important to him, but it's a valid point to bring up. Also, if a seller is not happy about giving you a lower interest rate than the current rate, explain to him your justification for asking for the lower rate. This seller has no overhead. He's not employing tellers, loan officers, secretaries, etc. He's not paying rent on a high-priced building or putting out expensive advertising. He does not need to charge the hefty interest rates of banks even at a lower rate. He will still do quite well financially.

The seller may walk away from you. Don't let this discourage you. You have not failed—this deal was simply not for you. As we've said before, do not fall in love with the property or let it control your offer. There will always be another house whose owner might be more flexible and more anxious to sell.

If your negotiations don't work out, always be nice to your seller. Assure him that you agree that the house is worth what he's asking but you simply cannot pay it. Explain that as an investor you must make deals that are acceptable to your monetary goals, otherwise all your hard work is for naught. Being polite is not just common courtesy. Your seller may change his mind later if he cannot sell his property and give that polite investor a call. Treat everyone as you would like to be treated—this is good business. Don't forget to leave him your business card.

You should have a couple of contracts with you whenever you go looking. You may want to leave some in your car; whether you are looking for houses to buy or not, you never know when an opportunity might present itself to you. If your verbal negotiations are successful, contract to buy the property but use a contingency clause if you like.

97

Clauses

You always want a way out of a deal if something turns up that makes you change your mind about the buy. Always put a contingency clause into your offer. There is no sense in making an offer on a house that you do not intend to go through with—you're wasting your time and the seller's time. These clauses are to be used only in case of unforeseen circumstances or to specify that some task must be done before the closing will take place. Make sure your seller is aware of these clauses.

An effective catchall contingency clause is one that says: "contingent upon my partner's approval." If you don't have a partner, then make it contingent upon your lawyer's or your accountant's approval. Then, if for any reason you or your partner decide that this home is not for you, you have a clause which will allow you to cancel your contract.

You may want to put a clause in the contract that states that you have the right to show the property to prospective tenants before the closing—the seller should give you a key in this case. This way you can put a renter in the day after you close on the property, and your new home will not sit there eating your dollars; somebody will be helping you with the payments from day one.

We sometimes ask that the owner agree to let us work on the property to get it ready to rent or sell before the closing. They usually agree to this. Be careful to put only your time into it at this point—do not put any money into the property before the closing. Clean and straighten it up, but save your cash expenditures until the property is actually yours.

You may need a contingency clause in your contract that requires the owner to have some work done on the house before closing. This can be very helpful and could get you a house that is in better condition.

We once bought a house that was so filthy and cluttered that there was only a path in the rubbish to the different rooms of the house. It was a horrendous mess with grease literally dripping from the cabinets in the kitchen. One of the bedrooms was so full of trash that we could not get the door open to look at it. For this house we put a clause in the contract that the purchase was contingent upon the seller's removal of all this filth (we worded it more politely). She did not have to actually clean it, but we insisted that she remove the debris. This woman and her son took eight truckloads of trash to the dump before we were satisfied.

Had we not put that clause in our contract, they probably would not have removed the clutter. You'll run into your share of houses like this yourself. Neglected homes can be great buys, but use a clause to save yourself some very unpleasant work that should have been done before the house was put up for sale. Always check the house a few days prior to closing to ensure that the contingency clause has been fulfilled.

Another important clause you may want to put in your contract is: "contingent upon adequate financing." If you're hoping to find some choice financing for your property and that financing does not work, you may need this escape. We have often been nervous about financing before. Fortunately, it's always worked out for us and we haven't had to use this clause. But such wording in your contract might make you feel more secure, especially on your first buy.

A very important clause in a contract is: "contingent upon mechanical inspection." You should have this in every contract you present. If you discover that the plumbing will take $1100 to repair and the electrical system needs to be completely redone, you can bow out.

The seller will probably agree to pay for part of the repairs found by an inspector. You, the buyer, pay for the inspection itself, because this inspection is protecting you (it usually costs about forty dollars). The inspector will check out the electrical, plumbing, heating, and cooling systems of a property. After following countless inspectors for three years as they go through our properties, we finally feel confident that we know what to check for in a home. After you have bought and sold many homes, you may feel that you, too, can perform these inspections yourself. But for now, go with a professional inspector. It could save you a great deal of money.

Do not worry about putting a clause in your contract about having a title search done. If you read your contract carefully, you will find this clause already in there.

We've talked about several contingency clauses. We should warn you that too many clauses in an offer to buy can kill a deal. Sellers become wary when they see more than a couple of clauses. Put a broad contingency clause in the contract, along with your inspection clause, and carefully consider whether you want to include any others. These clauses should never be the focal point of your conversation with the seller. As always, you should concentrate on the positive. You should exhibit a confident attitude—you've seen the house, you want to buy it, and you do not expect anything to go wrong.

Offers

While you were out shopping, if you found several houses you liked, don't be afraid to make offers on all of them. It is very unlikely that all of them will be accepted, and if they are it is not the end of the world by any means. If you've made sensible offers on bargain properties, then perhaps you should go through with all of the deals. If this is too scary for you, or financially unfeasible, you can always use your contingency clause to escape.

If the seller accepts your offer and the contract is signed, you are now ready to turn everything over to a good title company. They will perform a title search on the property and answer many of the questions a first buyer might have. If all goes well—if the mechanical inspection turns out all right and the title search reveals no ghosts—you can plan to close on the property at an agreeable time for both you and the buyer (you do not have to sign the contract in each other's presence). The title company will bring the closing papers and any papers concerning the house, and all you have to do is read them and sign your name. You are now an owner of an investment home, the first of many.

Pretty painless, huh? You were so afraid that something might go wrong, but it all went so smoothly. Your new property is going to appreciate in value, give you a positive cash flow, and save you bundles in taxes. How sweet it is!

CHAPTER EIGHT

Financing

T HERE IS A STORY about an elderly man who was nearing death. He called in his three sons and told each to put money into his casket as a sign of respect. Upon his death, the first son, a doctor, passed by the casket and dropped in a thousand dollar bill. The second son, an attorney, walked in and put in ten one hundred dollar bills. The final son paused at the casket, wrote a check for three thousand dollars, and removed his brothers' cash. He was a real estate investor and had learned to think creatively about financing.

The most confusing thing you will face in your first days as a real estate investor is the financing. To a beginning investor the words we toss about so blithely, like "leverage," "balloon mortgage," and "conventional financing," can sound intimidating. To help you understand financing better, we're going to devote an entire chapter to exactly what types of financing there are and where you can go to find financial help. Do not be overwhelmed by this subject. Review this chapter as slowly as you must in order to understand it well. Once you finish our introduction on financing, you'll be able to read other, more specialized books and understand this confusing subject.

We talked before about real estate being the only investment in which you can borrow other people's money to make your investments, and how you can take ownership of your investment while paying for only a fraction of it (or even for none of it!). In case that sounds too good to be true, believe us, it is true. Almost everyone borrows money to buy a home—very few people have the amount of cash it requires to buy a house or property. Can you imagine how long it would take you to save up $60,000 to buy a home? About thirty years, but by the time you have the money, your kids would all be grown and they wouldn't need a backyard to play in anyway. Also, the house that interested you would have tripled in price. Thus, most people turn to financing to buy their homes. Without financing the vast majority of people in this country would never be able to buy a home of their own. Financing allows a person to move into a home now, without having to pay the full amount. Lenders realize that you'll have the money to buy a home and they're willing to let you in now instead of later.

Lenders, of course, do not do this solely out of the goodness of their hearts. They're making a good living. They charge an interest rate that reflects what they're paying to use the money they loan to you. In 1979, with double-digit inflation, the interest rates that lenders charged soared out of sight. With these high interest rates on homes which were quite expensive in the first place, many people were left thinking that it was simply too expensive to purchase a home. (If you're expected to make a payment of $700 a month on your home—an amount that is not uncommon for many homes—you're left with very little money to buy groceries after all your other bills are paid.) It became difficult to qualify for a loan, and even more difficult to keep up with the payments. It used to be that young, newly married couples could afford to buy a home. Today, these young couples find it nearly impossible.

Sellers realize that many couples have been priced out of the market, but they still need to sell their homes and they're willing to do a great deal of negotiating to do so. It is this group of motivated sellers that you're looking for. With creative thinking, knowledge, and credit, the doors to ownership are open. All you have to do is walk through them.

SOME IMPORTANT TERMS

Before we jump into financing, we would like to explain some terms to you. You may have heard these words before, but perhaps you are a bit confused as to what they mean. We'll explain them here—make sure to check our glossary for any other words you're having trouble with.

Equity

Equity is the amount of money you have in your home that is yours outside of your debts. If you have a home on which you owe a $20,000 first mortgage and the home would sell for $65,000, then your equity in the home is $45,000. You can borrow against the equity in your home while you are still living in it—many investors do this. This is done by taking out a second mortgage.

If you can buy a home for an under-market price, you are buying "instant equity." For example, if a home has a fair market value of $70,000 and you buy it for $52,000, the very day you close on that property you have $18,000 of equity to your credit. When you sell that home, this equity, plus any other appreciation or payments that have been made on the mortgage, is yours. The attraction of equity is one of the main reasons people turn to real estate investing. Remember, though, that the equity you have in all of your homes goes on your financial statement as one of your assets.

Terms

As it may be somewhat confusing, we would like to explain the difference between a loan, a mortgage, a trust deed, and a lien. Many people use the terms interchangeably, but there are some differences you should know about.

A loan is simply that, a loan—somebody lends you money so you can buy what you desire when you don't have the money on hand at that time. A loan may or may not be backed by some type of collateral or security—when dealing with real properties, collateral or security is almost always required.

A mortgage is a type of a loan secured by property or personal valuables—if you stop paying what you owe on this loan, the person who made the loan has the right to take over the house or whatever personal property secured it.

A trust deed (or deed of trust) is a special type of mortgage. In many states trust deeds have become so popular that mortgages have become obsolete, although the term mortgage is still alive and well. In fact, a trust deed is frequently referred to as a mortgage—people are more comfortable using the word mortgage because it's familiar.

A lien is any type of claim against a property. Liens include mortgages, deeds of trust, assessments, and taxes. Assessments are best explained by an example. We once bought a home that was quite run down. The former owners had done nothing for the home whatsoever. We bought it and began our rehab and then learned that we owed $450 to the city! The city had been forced to come to the house and mow the lawn because the former occupants simply refused to do it. It had obviously been quite a job, because the bill had come to $450. The lien was in process but had not been filed, so it didn't get filed until after we owned the property. This was an assessment against the house—

assessments usually are fees the city or county charges a homeowner for putting in a new sidewalk, sewer, etc. (This story has a happy ending—we went to a city council meeting and were able to persuade them that after all the money we were putting into the house, this assessment should be waived. Thank heaven for that trusty scrapbook of ours!)

Taxes refer to property taxes, or federal income taxes. If the taxes are not paid, the IRS can take over your home or the county can sell it back for back taxes. Back taxes can add up to a considerable amount of money, and a tax lien is assessed against the property—not the owner.

You should be aware of any liens against a home because many liens will legally carry over to the new owner of a home. This is why title insurance is so important; the title company checks a home to make sure there are no liens against it for which a buyer would be liable, and the company very seldom misses anything—our experience was unique.

A balloon mortgage is one in which a loan starts out at a certain rate, but that rate is not guaranteed to stay constant; it will stay at that starting rate for a period of several years, then the balance of the loan must be paid off or a new loan written at whatever interest rate is available at that time. Do you see why they're called balloon mortgages? They're inflatable. If inflation and interest rates go up, so might the amount you pay per month if you have to rewrite the loan. This sort of loan is a bit risky for the buyer because he initially buys this home with a lower interest rate, but he could face a situation after a few years where he must either pay off the balance of the loan or refinance it at the current (probably higher) interest rate. If the going rate is high at that time, he could end up with monthly payments several hundred dollars per month higher than what he's accustomed to. If he cannot qualify for a new loan, he's in real trouble. This could be a nasty problem for a buyer, and, as an investor, you want to be cautious with balloon loans. They can be quite helpful in some cases though. You could get into a home with the initially low interest payments, fix up the home, and then refinance or sell it and pay off your loan before the interest rates go up.

Graduated interest rates are related to balloon mortgages. A graduated interest rate mortgage will start out with a rate lower than the prime rate, and then go up, usually on an annual basis. For instance, a loan might start out at eight percent for the first year, nine percent the next year, ten percent the following year and, on the fourth year, top out at twelve percent. These mortgages can be great to help you get into a home, but be aware of the payment you'll be making in four years at that top rate. Another problem with these loans is their use of negative amortization. That is simply another way of saying that you're losing equity instead of building it.

Leverage

What is the single most important tool used in the building of every major architectural masterpiece in history, one that will allow you to build a fortune from practically nothing? If you answered "the slave," you are way off track. The answer is the lever. Leverage gives the builder the power to move tons of stone with little effort; it is also the force that allows you to control $100,000 with little or none of your own money.

Leverage is what turns investors into millionaires. Let's use a few numbers to clarify this exciting principle: By putting $5,000 down on an $80,000 house, you are controlling an estate worth sixteen times your investment. If the house appreciates (goes up) in value by ten percent, how much does your investment increase?

Property value:
Original value $80,000
Increase (10 percent) $8,000
New value $88,000

Your investment:
Original investment $5,000
Increase $8,000
New equity $13,000

What happened here? Some of the terms and figures may be confusing, but you'll catch on quickly. Basically, as the property itself increased by only ten percent, you were able to take the entire gain of $8,000 and add it to your down payment of $5,000. So your $5,000 investment is now worth $13,000, an increase of 160 percent!

You can easily see that the less your original investment is, the higher your return will be. If you had put only $500 down on the same property, your return would still have been $8,000—a 1600 percent return! *That's leverage!* And if you bought the property with no money down at all, what would your return have been? To figure that one out, you would have to divide your $8,000 by zero; try that one out on your calculator—it can't be done. A mathematician would have trouble with that kind of problem, but we welcome an infinite return any day of the week. Ask your local banker if he has any savings accounts that offer an infinite return, or even a mere 1600 percent.

Obviously, real estate investors want to control the maximum amount of real estate possible. The greater the number of properties an investor controls, the more she has appreciating, and the more she is able to write off on her taxes. If you have $10,000 with which to begin your investing career, you will want to use as little of that $10,000 as possible on each of your properties. If you can buy five houses worth $40,000 each, using $2,000 for each of the down payments, you will have control of $200,000 worth of real estate. Or you could have used that $10,000 to buy one piece of property worth $100,000. Do you see how leverage can help you? Leverage can be the key to a successful investing career.

Now we will discuss the different forms in which these terms will appear.

Owner Financing

The easiest type of financing, as we have said before, is owner financing. When a property is owner financed, the owner "gives" you the money to buy his home. In effect, he himself loans you the money with which to buy his property. However, the owner never hands you any cash. He doesn't have that kind of money any more than you do. Rather, he trusts you to make monthly payments to him on his house—he will probably hold a deed of trust—and he'll get his equity back this way instead of in a lump sum. The seller can be happy with this arrangement because he'll have money coming in every month to help him pay his bills. If an owner needs cash right away, find out how much he needs. If that amount seems feasible to you, and the purchase still feels right, then give him the cash he wants as a down payment via conventional financing and have him finance the rest. We have found that combining conventional and owner financing strategies is a great way to make a deal work for everyone.

You can be very creative with owner financing. There are no limits to the methods you can use to pay for a property, using your negotiating power and leverage. With an owner as your lender, you can ask to have the loan that he is giving you structured so it fits your own needs. Perhaps you want your payments to be deferred for several months so you'll have time to improve the property and find tenants. Perhaps you want to structure your offer so you will have a greater positive cash flow at the beginning and a smaller one later. We have offered to pay eight percent interest for the first year, nine percent interest for the second, and ten percent for the remainder of the loan period. If graduated payments like this frighten you, then perhaps you could plan to amortize the loan over a different period of time so that the loan will be completely paid off rather than paying higher interest rates. With an owner providing the financing, you have much more control over the form of loan you receive. Don't be afraid to ask for the plan you want to meet your needs.

We're going to give you a couple of examples of the owner financed deals we've made, to help you understand the process better. Lynda was once giving a talk to a teacher's group on alternative careers. This was when we were all still teachers and just beginning to realize that our investments could allow us to give up teaching completely and make more money. After her talk, a teacher approached Lynda and asked if our partnership would buy any house.

"Yes," answered Lynda. "What do you have in mind?" This woman knew of a house that was so filthy that it could not be shown, and as a result it had been on the market for months. Lynda was accustomed to messy houses by now, and told the woman that all she looked at as she investigated a possible investment property were the walls, floors, ceilings, and windows. Lynda gave the teacher a card and told her to have the seller of the house give her a call. The seller called a few days later.

To make a long story short, the teacher hadn't been exaggerating. That house was one of the filthiest we had ever seen—it definitely ranks among the top five of our messiest buys. But the floor plan was great. The home had a large living room, a nice kitchen, three bedrooms, one and a half baths, a family room, and a garage—all of the things we like to see in a prospective buy. We knew the home had lots of potential, but it would also take lots of work. Though a tidy house with the same floor plan would have cost quite a bit more, we were able to pay only $41,000 for the home. We put $1,000 down and agreed to pay the owner $40,000 over a period of thirty years at a very reasonable interest rate.

We rehabilitated the home and rented it out as quickly as possible. We were not finished yet, however. None of us liked the idea of owing money to a person irresponsible enough to let his house fall apart, and we knew that we could have cash in our hands if we refinanced. It was time to negotiate again. We asked the owner if she would give us a discount on the amount we owed her if we paid the loan off immediately She agreed to give us a $2,500 discount if we gave her all her money in a bundle, so we agreed and then we went in search of new financing.

We went to the FHA and received a new loan on the property; processing and qualifying for this new loan took us eight months—nothing moves quickly when the federal government is involved. We paid off the owner, putting her out of the picture, and after her discount, the money we'd spent fixing the house up, and the down payment, we had a $9,000 profit, a paycheck we were all happy with.

The next home we bought didn't need much fixing up. It was a beautiful home, and we found that the owner had his loan all paid off—the house was his, free and clear. Well, from our real estate readings and seminars, we learned to pay close attention when we heard phrases like "free and clear." An added plus was that up until this time, the man had been having problems selling the house. We put together our most creative offer yet, using our leverage.

We offered him $50,000 for his house, and, as this was quite a bit less than what it was worth, we offered to give him a $25,000 cash down payment and asked him to take a $25,000 second mortgage on the apartment building we owned. This is what leverage is all about—using what you already hold the title on to help you buy even more properties.

We then went to the bank and easily received a $25,000 loan for this property (as it was worth almost triple that). We gave the owner his cash down payment and started making payments on that second mortgage. We didn't do much to the house—we recarpeted, painted, and cleaned up the yard. We put some tenants in there on a lease option for $650 a month—$100 of their payment was going toward their down payment. We then refinanced the house with another FHA loan. We received $53,000 from the FHA, and with this money we paid off the bank which had lent us $25,000 to make the down payment. We had $28,000 left over to put in our pockets, and we kept right on going, looking for other properties to buy.

Do you see what we did? We pulled the cash we used out of our apartments and put it to work for us, and yet we did not have to sell that first property—we cranked some cash. This experience is our answer to anyone who says that real estate holdings freeze up an investor's money. If you're creative, you can pull your equity out of your investment and make it work for you.

The next house we found was a nice ranch-style home, and it was also owned free and clear. It didn't take long for the lights to start flashing in our heads. We gave the owner $61,000 for the house with $2,000 down. He carried a $15,000 mortgage on the property. We took out second mortgages on two of our other properties and were the owners of another home. We'd used leverage once again to buy a home. We then started our search for refinancing. By this time our partnership's financial statement looked quite healthy, and we used it for the first time to apply for a loan through a bank. On the recommendation of several investors, we went to a very flexible banker. He moved quickly to appraise the home, and defined its market value at $65,000. He gave us a $53,000 mortgage on the house. Out of this, we paid the seller his $15,000 and had $38,000 left over to do whatever we wanted. We put it into our partnership and used it to buy more houses.

On the first of these transactions we made a profit of $9,000, on the second transaction we pocketed $28,000, and on the third we made $38,000. Remember that this was all borrowed money we took in and built our partnership on, and borrowed money is *tax free*. Can you see why we three school teachers quit our jobs and took up real estate investing full time? Our partnership was really starting to take off, suggesting that we spend all our time in real estate. We have never regretted our decision to take up investing as a full-time career. We doubt you will either, if this is what you choose to do.

By this time, we had a break-even cash flow, which is not as nice as a positive cash flow, but we had lots of money in the bank. Once we had given up our teaching jobs, we spent forty hours a week shopping for homes and making offers.

We had each put only $4,000 of our own money into this venture in the first place. With all the homes we were buying and the equity we were building, we were using somebody else's money. In our minds, because we don't use our own money, these are "nothing-down" deals. The seller does receive a down payment, but these down payments do not come out of our bank accounts. Of course, we were paying to use the money, but our names are on the titles to these properties and not someone else's; we reap all the tax benefits on the investments and we can use them as tools to buy other properties. And, in twenty years or so, many of these properties will be paid off. We can either sell them or continue renting them out and add that money to our meager social security checks.

Wraparound Mortgages. Sales.

We have not talked about the wraparound mortgage. We call it a wraparound when the owner "wraps" a new loan around his previous mortgage. For example, a seller has his home for sale at $50,000. After negotiating, you give him $5,000 down and, as he is willing to finance the property himself, he gives you a $45,000 mortgage at twelve percent for thirty years. You, the buyer, are paying $463 (without taxes or insurance) a month to the seller. The owner has a loan still in place on the house and he continues to pay on it rather than let you take it over. He owes $20,000 with fifteen years of payments remaining— his payments are $200 per month on that first mortgage. He continues making those payments with the money you're giving him and has about $263 every month left over to put into his bank account. He's happy—someone is making his mortgage payment and giving him extra cash to play with. You're happy—you are going to place a renter in the home who makes your mortgage payment for you and leaves you with some extra cash while your equity is growing.

We are not afraid of these wraparound buys; in fact, we actually prefer them to some of the other kinds of financing available. In a wraparound situation you hold the deed to the property, while in another popular form of financing, the contract-for-deed (or CFD), the seller retains the deed until the contract is paid off. We feel safer with the deed in our possession. We do ask, however, in our wraparound deals that the payments be escrowed by someone whose credentials are agreeable to both parties, which usually means a bank. In that case, we make our payments to the bank and the bank makes the payments to the owner. There is a small charge for this service, but the peace of mind it buys is well worth it.

You really deserve a pat on the back for having dared to start buying investment properties. Remember, you do not need money, you need *credit*. Much of our economy is just a confidence game, and as long as big businesses, corporations, all have confidence in one another and in the government of the United States, the game continues. Money flows in a big circle from institution to institution, a constant stream of money. Don't stay outside this circle—jump in! You can learn to play the confidence game as well as everyone else. You, too, should take an active part in making those leading economic indicators go up.

Conventional Loans

We have talked so far about owner-financed deals. Usually, we refinance these owner-financed properties with loans through a mortgage company, but most of our buys started out without the involvement of a bank at all. A bank will offer you a conventional loan, as will a savings and loan, a finance company, or a mortgage company. Some investors dislike the conventional loan process intensely because of the rigid credit requirements and the tendency of most banks to be less than creative. Thus, many investors completely ignore such institutionally-financed loans.

However, you may be like us; you may want to go through a bank for refinancing at times. Or maybe you have found a home that is going into foreclosure and you need some cash to pay off the mortgages against it so you can buy it for a fraction of its market cost. Conventional loans *are* within your reach, once you have improved your credit rating. Remember that loan companies and banks want to lend people money; this is how they make money. A loan officer must be cautious, however, because his superiors are not at all happy when a loan backfires. So take a positive attitude, and once you feel that your credit rating is convincing enough, go for it. Apply for your loan!

But what if you run into an obstacle? What if you have gone to a bank, fully prepared with your financial statement, profit and loss statement, scrapbook, partnership papers, all of your figures and plans for the property . . . and you find out after the application has gone to the loan committee that they have turned you down?

Believe it or not this does happen. It has even happened to us. Some banks are conservative, and they may not make it a practice to make the sort of loan you are asking for. Do not fret or be discouraged, not even for a minute. Keep your head held high and go directly to the competition. If they refuse you, too, keep right on going. Find a bank with an eye to the future, a bank that will give you a loan.

If you are rejected by a bank, don't accept it without a word. You have something to learn here. Go back to that bank, in person, and find out exactly why you were turned down. What didn't they like in your presentation? Is it bank policy to refuse this type of loan application, or did you leave something out as you spoke with the loan officer? If it was a mistake on your part, don't make that mistake again. More likely, though, the problem lies in the lending institution's conservative policies.

We once knew a very determined woman who was turned down by nine banks before she found one that would give her a loan. She finally found a bank that would cooperate with her, and went on to buy her homes. You may have to swallow rejections at first, but never give up. And do not take a bank's rejection of a loan as a rejection of you personally. All of your dealings with banks are business dealings only—they are never refusing you on the grounds of your looks and your personality. It is not fun to have a bank turn down your loan application, but neither is it the end of the world, not by any stretch of the imagination.

Ask your investor and realtor friends if they know of any lending institutions or loan officers who think as creatively as you do. And once you've found such a banker, never let him go. As we said before, make sure he sees you bring in all your money transactions to that bank—never go through the Drive-Thru window. There you are, successful, efficient, and happy with your ventures. He'll notice this. Come to know the tellers, customer service people, and secretaries. You are helping to pay their paychecks by borrowing money from that bank! And they are helping you by giving you money to buy your homes. If your banker is accustomed to seeing you and realizes just how successful you are, he may just give you a call if the bank ends up taking a home back in a foreclosure. Connections are vital in this business, with your lenders as well as everybody else.

Once you have bought a few homes, you'll have an impressive financial statement to flaunt, and lenders will be very happy to see you. For your first few investments, if your credit rating doesn't look strong, buy through owner financing, and refinance later using your knowledge to pull some cash out of your property.

FHA and VA

Let's talk about FHA and VA loans. FHA stands for the Federal Housing Administration; VA stands for the Veterans' Administration. The FHA and VA are run and regulated by the U.S. government. Our country is unique in having such organizations to insure or guarantee loans so its citizens can buy homes. Ask a European how many people in his country own homes and where he lives. His answer will likely be, "In a rented apartment." There are more private home owners in the U.S. than in any other country in the world. The FHA and VA, to a great extent, are responsible for this.

With an FHA deal you must go through a mortgage or a savings company to get your money. You must qualify for your loan; this qualifying process can take quite a long time. The FHA is thus not a financing method to use if you need money in a hurry. But these loans do have the advantage of being fairly easy to assume. You pay only a nominal transfer fee and the seller doesn't have to meet any requirements at all. FHA and VA loans are extremely attractive to us when we're shopping. They are fixed rate and easily assumable for us, and future buyers as well.

The FHA will insure any loan it makes to a qualified buyer. If an owner who bought his home through the FHA fails to make his payments and loses the home in a foreclosure, the FHA will take over the home. The FHA prints a list of these foreclosed properties, and you as an investor should ask your realtor for a copy.

The FHA loans for investment can be expensive these days because of constantly narrowing restrictions. When you want to borrow $70,000 and the interest rate is fourteen percent, you're talking about a high monthly payment. The qualifying process takes too long for these loans to be as popular as they were in the past. To spend all that time waiting to see if you qualify, just to be rejected, can be very discouraging. Even if you qualify, the FHA can be a frustrating way to go. If we had waited for some of our bargain buys to be qualified for a loan through the FHA, those properties would have been gone. For this reason we have used FHA loans for refinancing only. We try to get into our homes with bank financing or owner financing.

If you're a veteran, you can use your VA eligibility. VA loans go through banking institutions just as FHA does, but the VA guarantees those loans and the rate of interest is attractive. The VA helped put thousands of World War II vets into homes and is therefore greatly responsible for this country's postwar boom. The beauty of a VA loan is that in using it you don't have to put any money down. There is no lengthy qualifying process, and if a home that was bought through the VA goes into foreclosure, the VA is responsible for it and will pay the loan off. To buy a home using VA benefits, it must be your residence. The VA does not make investment loans unless you purchase a property from them on which they have foreclosed.

When you find a home with an old VA or FHA loan that is assumable, this is certainly a point in favor of buying the home. Those interest rates are fixed and very attractive in comparison to today's loans.

Use any government agencies available to you for help in purchasing your home. Call HUD—Housing and Urban Development—and ask them any questions you have. They often know about special loans available for low-income buyers. Watch your newspaper's housing section—lists of available special loans can be found there. Talk with people—there are many agencies to help you, and many prospective investors are not even aware of their existence.

Other Sources

If you're short of money to buy a home and are having little luck, there are alternatives you may not have thought of. Do you have a life insurance policy? What is its cash value? Are you aware that you can borrow money against your insurance policy? You pay a low interest rate on this money, because it is your own money—six to eight percent is the common rate. This is a fantastic deal because while you're borrowing at this low percentage rate, your insurance policy is earning money for you at ten to twelve percent or so, depending on your policy. You can take this money at a very low interest rate, make a down payment on a property, and yet still be earning interest on the money you borrowed!

Do not worry about whether you are still covered or not—of course you are. In the unlikely event that something happens and you don't wake up tomorrow, your insurance policy will pay off your beneficiaries. Pulling money out of your insurance policy is just like using a home as leverage to receive more cash—just as you still hold title to the home, your insurance policy is still intact. You have merely taken out some of the money you've put into it, that's all.

Another alternative in looking for your down payment money is your own purse. How many major credit cards do you have? What is your credit limit on these cards? A thousand dollars on each? If you have two cards, you have enough to make a down payment on a house. Pull your money out and put it down; start making your house payments and charge-card installments and you're on your way.

Using Your Equity

Another place to acquire money for your investments is the house you're presently living in, if you own it. You can pull the equity out of your own home and use it as a down payment to buy another property. Put a second mortgage on your home to get at the cash you've put into it and go shopping. Sometimes a seller will even accept a note drawn against your home. Instead of asking the seller to carry a mortgage secured by the home he is selling you, ask him to carry the note secured by your own residence. When he agrees, go to the stationery supply store, buy a note, and type in the terms you have agreed upon. You'll be sure to make every payment on time because you certainly don't want to lose your own home, and the seller knows this. You'll find it very easy to refinance the property you have bought from the seller because there's no mortgage on that property, and you have plenty of *tax free* money to go shopping.

In our investing, we haven't actually used the method above—money from our own homes. Each of us put $4,000 of our own borrowed money into this partnership and chose not to use the equity from her home. Many investors have fully mortgaged their homes and bought several more homes with the money. To own a home free and clear is a foolish crime as far as they're concerned—they think the money tied up in your home should be used to buy yet more homes. Each investor must establish his or her own goals for investing. There is no right and wrong in investing. Numerous fully leveraged properties are certainly beneficial if you think in terms of appreciation. Twenty homes valued at $50,000 will make you $2,500 each per year in appreciation alone if you consider a five percent appreciation rate. That increases your financial statement by $50,000 in one year if you own this hypothetical set of properties. In addition to this, a portfolio of twenty $50,000 fully leveraged properties probably would keep Uncle Sam from dipping into your hip pocket as well.

You may feel you could not sleep at night being fully leveraged. Perhaps you feel you'd be a nervous wreck and have to check into the funny farm. If this is your personality, then possibly owning fewer, but free and clear, properties is your goal. Find your own threshold for risk and invest within your own limits.

Our own goal was to put as little of our own money as possible into this venture. And we have stuck with this policy. Call us foolishly cautious if you care to, but we feel that we've done very well in spite of the fact that we left our personal equities alone. Instead we pull equities out of our other income properties to buy new ones.

Assumptions

As we said earlier, if you can find a home on one of your shopping trips that claims to be assumable with a exciting price tag, make sure you take a close look at it. Some loans—conventional, FHA, VA, or whatever—have interest rates as low as five or six percent. In most cases you'll have to come up with other financing to meet the asking price, but you can work this out with the owner. You could either give him his equity in monthly payments, or get a second mortgage to pay him off completely.

Lease Option

With all of these methods available to you to purchase a home, you should be able to find one that will meet your needs. But if you're still having problems and feel that a lease option is your best bet, go ahead. It may prove a great first move for you. Be sure to agree that you have the right to sublet your property.

Some suggestions for the individual who sees her only choice as leasing with an option: this technique has many benefits you may not have considered. You must negotiate your option just as you would a purchase. Negotiate the longest possible term for your option at the lowest price you can agree upon. Even though you do not actually own the property, you receive all the appreciation over the period of your option. The property will appreciate if you manage and maintain it well.

Negotiate the lowest possible rent you can. One way to do this is to agree that you'll handle all maintenance and will never call the owner. You might negotiate an additional discount if your rent is always on the first of each month. When you sublet your fixed-up property you may have a nice positive cash flow.

The only benefit you will not receive with an option is income tax benefit. But there is no reason why a woman, even a woman on welfare, can't use this technique to better her life-style! The lease and option agreement must be a well-written agreement. Never rely on verbal agreements!

Financing is not an easy subject to understand. It is something understood with time—don't feel discouraged and confused.

Give yourself time to become familiar with this new terminology. Any time you start to feel overwhelmed with any of the books, lists, or contracts you read, stand up, stretch, and take a walk. Clear your mind and try again later. We have given you a rudimentary explanation of financing. Your library offers a vast supply of books with techniques. You'll be surprised at just how many different ways there are to structure your offers with the different types of financing available.

CHAPTER NINE

Rehabilitation: *Wallpaper* and Other Magic Tricks

F EELING GUILTY because you missed your twenty-minute workout for the 360th day in a row? Wish you looked a little more like Jane Fonda? Planning to begin your exercise program after the holidays? Have we got a workout for you! You can forget all those guilt trips, drag out your comfy old grubbies, and make thousands while you exercise!

Once you own your home, it may need some work. This can be scary for beginning investors. In this chapter we're going to try to help you deal with the idea of cleaning and decorating yet another home.

We've discussed some of the nasty cleaning and rehab jobs we have done. Honestly, we've had some of our best times while fixing up a house. We talk about every subject under the sun as we scrub and paint, and we spend a lot of time laughing. It's not that bad—with a partner, it's even fun. We totally transform a house in poor condition, making it into a livable home. Our greatest pleasure is using our creativity in redecorating a home, leaving it charming, for a small amount of money. It is a constant challenge to all of us to improve a house as economically as possible in order to attract someone quickly to start making our payments for us. Such mental work is exhilarating and rewarding.

Our rehabs have also added to our confidence. How many women do you know who can rip up a tile floor and glaze a window? How many men do you know who can redecorate a home with $300 and make it look as if they'd put ten times that much into it? We see ourselves very differently now. We were not especially handy around the house before we started, but we've learned a

117

lot in these past few years and now we're equal to almost any task. We are not afraid of leaky faucets, and even roaches don't send us screaming out the door. We can do tasks that are stereotypically men's work, and many times we do them even better. It's a great feeling to break out of roles and prove ourselves.

Our children even look at us differently. For the past few years our kids have watched us take these houses that need quite a bit of money put into them and re-do them into charming homes. Lynda has two sons: Do you think they're going to grow up thinking that a woman's talents around the house come to a stop after she's cleaned up? Those boys have watched Lynda tear down cabinets and re-caulk windows. All of our children, whatever their sex, have realized that women have the potential to do anything they set their minds to. It's a good lesson for any child to learn.

Our children have also learned how to do some minor repair work. We can finish up more quickly when a gang of ten people storm a messy home together. Even our youngest helper—a five-year-old—has learned to take up a floor and paint the inside of a closet by himself. We've put several of the kids in a room by themselves with some paint, brushes, a pizza, and some drinks, and been pleased with the results (even if they did get a bit carried away at times with the ceiling and windows). And to make it an even more important learning experience for them, we pay them for their efforts. We took them on a vacation one summer in payment for all their work and had a terrific time. These are good experiences for children. They're learning how to do basic maintenance around the home, and to be responsible. They're also learning the business from the ground up by sharing the work and rewards. There's a great deal of phone answering and message taking that the children can do. Jane pays her daughters for their help, which gives the girls spending money and Jane a tax deduction.

As you can see, we do not mind rehab work. As long as the three of us are working together, it's endurable and even enjoyable. We think it could be this way for you too. Take your kids! Your dog! Your portable music makers! Meet your partners (if you have any) at the house and promise yourselves a great dinner at the end of the day! It can be a proper outing, if you're determined that it can be fun.

When we first shop for a home, we estimate the cost and the time we must devote to the property's rehabilitation. We have a budget and a list of priorities for the project. When we began, we lacked the knowledge to estimate how much the major jobs would cost, but after receiving a few professional estimates and always shopping carefully for supplies, we've learned how much things cost. Now we can also decide whether we'll have some of the work done by others. We decide what jobs we intend to do ourselves, and what we'll contract to have done.

Once we buy a property—and after the closing has taken place—we set definite dates for when we're going to have this home finished, and call in an ad to our paper so we can start receiving calls on the house right away. This deadline makes us hustle to make that house shine as soon as possible. We usually plan three weeks for a major rehab and a shorter amount of time on jobs that require less work. Some projects only require one afternoon.

We don't much like it when we have to extend our deadlines. We make those deadlines for a reason: we want to start making money on those homes right away, and when we don't meet deadlines, our plans are delayed. There's nothing worse than a vacant property; it's nothing but a baby alligator gobbling up dollars. So once we do have our rehab plans and deadlines, we put all our efforts into the house and we fly to get finished! We recommend that you do the same. Know what you are going to do and know your priorities, set up your time frame, and go to it. Stick to your rehab plans—what job to do when, how much money to spend on it, etc. Allow no random changes in your rehab schedule. This will only extend the amount of time you'll be working on the property. Do not procrastinate, not even for one day. Procrastination is for people with a guaranteed paycheck from an employer, not for an adventurous and self-employed real estate investor.

Go To It!

"Oh my gosh, they accepted. The closing is over, they have my money and now I own this dirty house. What in the world do I do now?" First thing: remain calm. We have put this off long enough, it's time to pack up and begin your project.

Go to your closet and dig out your grubbiest clothes and attack this task head on. We have rather fancy grubbies. One year just before Christmas our husbands took us out to a lovely restaurant for dinner. After dinner they were planning to present us with our gifts. Suddenly three of the waitresses appeared, wearing green overalls with rainbow lettering. On the back was printed our company's name and on the front over the pocket, our names. We received two different pairs—a light pair for warm weather and an insulated pair for the winter months. We also received a cordless electric drill. We were thrilled to pieces and everyone seated at nearby tables thought our presents were great. We really utilize our overalls. They're perfect to wear over nice clothing. We often find we must work a portion of our day on a rehab, then race off to the bank. We just slip off our overalls, change shoes, and we're ready to meet our banker. They're really super.

Don't forget your camera; you want to take your "before" photos for your scrapbook. Now, on to the property. Take many photos of it as is, both outside and in. We encourage you to use our scrapbook idea. It saved us $450 once, which certainly made it well worth the small cost and effort. The scrapbook is especially important for women. We take it with us whenever we're trying to establish ourselves with a new bank. Sometimes it's difficult for a lender to believe that we know what we're doing without evidence from some of our projects. We take pictures of each of us doing the work so the banker knows we really did it. We also keep wallpaper and paint samples and put them on the pages with the pictures.

Before we begin rehab, we take an inventory of needed supplies. Time spent in preparation at this point means many hours saved in the long run. Arrive with boxes, trash sacks, tools, ladders, and gloves. Take care of the trash first—remove any trash, old bushes, or weeds. Go through one room at a time, discarding all the trash and anything else that you don't want. You'll probably find something that can be useful—old bookshelves that could look nice with new varnish, tables to store tools in your garage, etc. Never toss out any curtain rods—it's nice to have a few extras around.

We learned the hard way that it's a good idea to keep all trash in tidy boxes and not overload your trash bags. We once piled up unusable carpeting, boxes, and trash bags in a heap at the curb to haul away the next day, and that night it rained buckets. What a soggy mess! And we were the lucky ones who got to clean it up. We now try to keep all this junk manageable. Trash is a continual problem in the rehab business. Organized trash will make your new neighbors happier too.

Speaking of neighbors, we always introduce ourselves to them. They're usually thrilled to have someone improving the property, and they become very interested in our work. These neighbors can provide many services. They keep an eye on your vacant property (usually loaded with tools), can recommend someone for yard work, and know about trash service in the area. They may even let you use their telephone when you need it!

These same neighbors will also call you if your renter is a problem or if he moves out after you've leased the home.

If you decide that you want to economize and take your own trash to the dump (it will cost you under ten dollars while somebody else will charge about thirty), prepare yourself. If you're like us, you have probably never been to the dump before. On our first major rehab, we got our chance. We took two truck loads to the city dump. We weren't sure that we'd make it—even though we had the trash tied down, it seemed bound to fall off. But off we went on the thirty mile trek (dumps are always a long way away—they aren't popular sites to have close to a city). The trip was an experience—the dirt roads were muddy and we slid all over them. But we made it with all of our trash, and we unloaded it, knee deep in mud and flies. We laugh about this trip now, but at the time we were anxious to get the job over with and leave. We never made that trip again—we hire all trash removal now!

We were very lucky with another major rehab. The city was so pleased we were rehabilitating a property that had been a problem for a long time that they sent a huge dump truck over and left it overnight for us to load. The next morning they hauled it away for us free of charge. If your city is aware that you're rehabilitating a property that has been an eyesore for years, they just might help you out too.

Once you've cleared your property of all debris, it's time to consider your priority list. Certain jobs, if they're done before others, make your rehab flow more smoothly. Prepare all your walls for painting with spackle, if it's needed. Get your new bathrooms and kitchens functioning first. Spray paint the ceilings if they need it. Next do the plumbing, electrical, doors, and moldings. Tasks such as these should all be done before any carpet is laid or final coats of paint go on the walls. You will save time and money this way. It takes time to learn the best order for tasks. We've made many mistakes in this area and learned from our mistakes.

Curb Appeal

One of your highest priorities should be curb appeal. By curb appeal, we mean how the home looks from the outside. If a prospective tenant or buyer drives up and does not like the way the outside looks, chances are he'll keep right on driving and will never step foot inside your property. If there's trash all over the yard, or it's overgrown with weeds, you're going to have to clean it up. Perhaps you put a clause in your contract that the seller must cut back the weeds and haul away debris. Do any mowing, trimming of bushes, and cleaning of the yard that's necessary. We have found that little touches like shutters on the windows add personality to a home. And they're inexpensive as well.

121

We have bought sets on sale for ninety-nine cents. We buy the shutters first so we can match the trim paint to them. We have also found that astro-turf on the front porch works wonders in covering ugly cracks in cement and gives a fresh look to the home. We buy big wooden numbers that will match the trim, and display the address in a cheery way—it also makes the property easier to locate for those coming to look at it.

Use your creativity on the outside. What little touch would make it look better? Perhaps you need to add an attractive mailbox. How good are you with flowers? Everyone likes flowers. We have built flower boxes, painted them to match the house, and put geraniums or chrysanthemums in them. We have changed spindles on the porch railing to give the home a newer look, or replaced a modern railing and put in an older style to match an older home. (Remember that old, renovated homes are all the rage in many parts of the country now.) These little touches add thousands of dollars to the value of the home.

The choice of exterior color is always based on the current state of the exterior paint. Is the base already an acceptable color? Perhaps the paint job is fine but boring. If the paint is in good shape we choose a new trim color to accent what is already there. Perhaps we use maroon trim on a gray house or hunter green on a white house, but we don't repaint unless necessary.

If the house truly needs a total paint job, we usually use from three to five compatible colors on the front, usually earth or neutral tones. (We avoid avant-garde splashes of vivid green and outrageous orange.) We use a semi-gloss base for the entire house and a gloss paint for the trim. This gives our homes a crisp, clean appearance.

A bit of advice: keep your eye on the weather as you paint. Once when we had to paint the outside of a home, we used our brand-new airless spray gun. We were so proud of our work and so impressed with that spiffy little paint gun of ours that we did not take a look around us to see what the weather was doing. Well, a cloud must have been impressed with our sprayer, too, because one arrived overhead to find out more about it. On reaching our property, that cloud dumped water all over our brand new paint job. Luckily, two walls were dry enough and weren't harmed, but the other two were rinsed clean. When you're working on the outside of your home, do look up every now and then.

Rain can cause other problems as well. With one house, every time it rained, an inch or more of mud would wash up into the garage. We couldn't figure out what the problem was until we were there during a storm and noticed that our slanted driveway was acting as a riverbed, dumping water and mud into the garage. This was not a big problem for us—we simply dug a little ditch to catch the water. We put some grating over it so cars could drive across, and now there's no problem at all.

Remember, as you clean and decorate, the things you would like to see in a home. You are decorating for women, and they like a tidy, attractive appearance outside. So do men, for that matter, if they stop to consider it. Always keep in mind the people who will be moving into your house.

You have already cleaned your property, now take a good look around the inside. What does this house need? You have already decided that the bathroom needs help, but what exactly is wrong with it? Does it need a new toilet seat, a new sink? What would be the most sensible expenditure you could make on this home? As you're thinking about this, keep in mind the rooms most important to improve—the bathroom and kitchen. Buy items for those rooms first. Ask yourself if each expenditure will truly make the home more appealing.

Maybe this house of yours is a classic case as far as clean-up goes; perhaps, although the trash is gone, there are some small visitors that must be taken care of. Roaches, fleas, and other pests should be dealt with before any redecorating work is done. Don't be frightened by these little tenants. We've fought them all, and we won. You can do it too. A comforting thought when dealing with such varmints is the size difference between the two of you. You are at least a hundred times bigger, and while you can simply swat at one to send it flying, it would take thousands of them to carry you very far (do not concentrate on this image too much). You have the advantage here because you're taller and capable of rational thought and battle strategies; they're mere insects, not even aware that they're targets for annihilation.

We are not saying that it's easy to rid yourself of such pests; we were almost defeated by them once ourselves. We bought a home for $23,000 and allotted ourselves only $300 in rehab money—we were low on cash reserves—ah, those early days. . . . After closing on this property, we visited it very briefly and saw bugs everywhere! We only stayed long enough to spray insecticide, and then locked up.

A few days later we returned, sure our problem would be solved. The pests were still going strong! We sprayed again, this time with a more noxious poison. We left the can in the middle of the kitchen floor as a warning to the bugs that their days were numbered, and again left.

The third time we returned to the property, we found those horrid little cockroaches holding a meeting on top of our spray can! We gave up trying to kill them ourselves and hired an exterminator. We stayed right there in the house and cleaned them up.

If you're ever dealing with fleas, try wearing knee socks to keep your ankles bite-free. We once had a home that was full of fleas, and Jane discovered that heavy knee socks were the way to win with them. In that same home, we kept spraying for fleas but they just wouldn't go away. We couldn't figure out what the problem was. Finally, one day we noticed the door to the crawl space was missing. We replaced it. Apparently, a dog had been coming onto the property for some free lodging after we left each night, and was leaving his tiny friends behind for us to deal with. Once we replaced that door and sprayed a few more times, we were free from any more flea problems.

If you live in a part of the country that has lots of insect problems, you may want to find a dependable exterminator for your four-legged crawlers. They won't be happy with this, but you can't expect everyone in your new neighborhood to like you.

The Wonders of Wallpaper and Other Hints

It takes so little to make a house look so much better. A fresh coat of paint, a dash of wallpaper, and trimming touches can make all the difference in the world. None of these additions costs much, if you know where to shop and what to buy. This will come with time. Your first house could be the one on which you spend the most money. (It certrainly will prove to be the one that keeps you up most at night.) By the time you buy your fifth home, you will probably learn to be not quite so particular, adjust to the fact that this is not your own personal home, and have less trouble purchasing a less expensive door lock, hinge, faucet, etc. Experience is a great teacher and it will come to you—we promise.

Paint

We choose neutral colors for the inside because these are appealing to most people. We use an off-white latex enamel that does both walls and wood-work, and we use the same shade on every property. This way, if the tenants move out and there is touch up to be done, we know exactly what color the paint is and always have some on hand. This will save you a lot of money—you aren't going out to buy new paint all the time and tossing out half a can that isn't useful anymore is wasteful.

Check with several paint stores that sell good quality paint, and since you're going to be buying all your paint there, ask for a discount on your purchases.

If an owner is unwilling to do this, you may want to go somewhere else. As we recommended before, set up an account at the paint store. Charging paint and wallpaper gives you thirty days on someone else's money.

Buy only good quality paint. In our early days as investors, we thought we could save some money by using less expensive paint. This was not true—we actually ended up spending more money this way. With cheap paint you need to put on two or three coats, which is very costly in both time and money. Call a few house-painting companies and ask them which type of paint they use. Make them more happy to speak with you be confiding that you're an investor who will paint this first property yourself, but plan on contracting your paint jobs in the future. Once you have a few opinions, you'll be ready to start buying your paint.

Wallpaper

Wallpaper is one of the best friends you can have in this business. Wallpaper makes a room look more spacious and adds a touch of class and personality. When an interested party walks in, he sees more than barren and boring walls on all four sides. This really does make a difference. In the kitchen especially we can take a dull and dreary place for preparing meals and make it into a cheery and charming room full of potential for fabulous food fixings. Wallpaper is your most important ingredient. If we don't paper a whole wall, we put a border around it. We don't purchase border wallpaper; it's too expensive. Instead we buy a roll of wallpaper from which we can cut a border and we work with that.

By shopping carefully you can find a store that sells wallpaper for only ten to twenty percent above cost, or a surplus store that has bins full of paper that sell for even less. These are great places to make your wallpaper purchases. If our house is to be a rental, we always buy washable, very study wallpaper. This will keep us from redecorating after our tenants move out.

Keep your eyes open for wallpaper bargains from your own home. Lynda removed a whole roomful of brown vinyl wallpaper with polka dots. It came down without a scratch, so we used it on some of our properties. Wallpaper that she would have otherwise thrown away is now in our homes all over the city.

We've made some homes sparkle with very little money—this is a magic ability that most women have, even though you may not be aware of it. Use your talents to turn a house into a home. Women can do a bit here and a bit there and a house will look wonderful.

Let's review what we've said by returning to that $300 rehab again to explain just how a little goes a long way. For this house we bought one gallon of hunter-green paint and changed a boring, white house by putting dark green trim around each window. We painted the door the same color. We also built flower boxes under the windows, a homey touch. We found an old milk can and painted it green to match the house and planted some flowers in it as well. We chose this color because it matched the shutters and a matching flower box. We found some spindles at a thrift store for $1.99 apiece and added a railing to the front porch. We added our large wooden house numbers and painted the mailbox. We covered the old wooden porch with green astro turf. The outside, for a very small investment, looked like a dollhouse. We thoroughly cleaned the inside and put up some gingham wallpaper above the kitchen cabinets. We painted two bedrooms and wallpapered the bathroom.

As you can see, our biggest expenditure on this home was our time. It needed to be cleaned and cared for more than anything else. It does not cost much money to scrub, trim bushes, mow, and haul away tons of trash. It just takes labor—your labor, if you are trying to save money.

When we had spent all of our $300 allotment, Jane, our numbers expert, made us quit. We then leased that home with an option to buy and we had a $150 positive cash flow per month after our bills were paid. A year later we sold it for $39,950. Do you remember what we paid for that home? Twenty-three thousand dollars. What a great feeling to make that much profit so quickly and so easily! This was almost a 600 percent return on our investment of $3,000. It was our hard work and frugal redecorating that made this possible.

Another house that we're proud of is the one for which Jane only allowed us ten dollars for rehabilitation. The house did not need much work; we knew this when we bought it. But still, ten dollars is not much to work with. But where there's a will, there's a way, and we found the way. With that ten-dollar bill we bought a pint of light yellow paint for the kitchen cabinets. We bought ninety-nine cent, rust-colored shutters for the all-important curb appeal, and some wax for the hardwood floors. That was it! Our rehab money on that house was all used up!

We put a lot of elbow grease into this home—we mowed, trimmed, washed walls, and scrubbed floors until they shone. We even used some of Lynda's old wallpaper. All of our work paid off—that ten-dollar rehab turned out to be one of our best investments. We rented the property for $440 per month, which easily covers our $260 mortgage payment. A $180 positive cash flow per month on ten properties would free almost any woman from having to work, don't you think?

Floor Coverings

Floor coverings are important. For homes that we hope to sell in a hurry without renting, we put in a plush or semi-plush rich neutral-tone carpet installed over a pad. We hire a professional to do this. We happen to have a friend in the business and can usually purchase carpet worth sixteen dollars a yard for nine dollars—including installation. Connections are wonderful.

If you don't have such friends, look for bargains whenever you can. If you tell a carpet shop you plan to be putting lots of carpet into lots of properties, the salesman may be very accommodating and give you a discount if you promise to come back. If you look in the classified ads of your newspaper, you'll find some good buys on used carpeting. A friend of ours, who was redecorating her home, recently found beautiful carpet through a decorator for $100—that was the total price for 750 square yards! Offices, hotels, and home owners are always redecorating in your city—shop around for what they discard.

For our rentals we use a neutral, multicolor, rubber-backed carpet. This doesn't show spots, and it's easy to care for and much less expensive to purchase, install, and maintain. If you wish to lay your own carpet, you can purchase your own tack strip, rent the kick tool, and install it yourself. Ask about these at a carpet shop.

We sometimes put carpeting in the kitchen and bath, but we usually use vinyl flooring. If we ever put vinyl over a large area, we hire a professional. He will lay the sub-flooring and the vinyl, and no wrinkles will ever show up later. We let him do the measuring, but we do the shopping to make sure we get a good price.

Windows

If you're buying homes in old neighborhoods, you might have trouble with the windows. These older windows depend on ropes and weights to move up and down—you may have to replace these if the windows do not open easily. Do it before painting.

To replace the weights in the window, remove the trim molding and the window itself. Now look on the inside of the wooden sash—the sash next to the window—and you'll find the sash in two pieces held together with screws about ten inches from the sill. Remove these screws and take the lower piece of wood out. You'll be able to see the weight. It's quite heavy and usually about ten inches long and two inches in diameter.

On each side of the window frame you have removed, you'll find a hole and a track for the sash rope. Be certain to purchase sash rope at your hardware store because sash rope won't stretch. You'll need to measure the length of the sash. For the correct measurement, begin at the middle of the window. Measure to the top and then down the entire length of the window (top and bottom). Allow enough rope for the knots and a little extra—about three inches. Cut your rope and tie a knot in one end. Lay the window on its side and insert the knot into the hole on the window's side frame. Run the rope up the track. Secure the knot by hammering a thin three-quarter-inch nail through the knot and onto the frame. Put the window back in place and thread the ropes through the wheels at the top of the sash and down behind the sash molding. As you do this, have a helper raise and hold the window so the rope will thread down to the opening at the bottom where you found the weights. Attach the weights to the sash ropes with a knot and replace the wood and screws. Then replace the window and the trim board, making sure it is snug against the windows again. If this trim board is too snug, the window won't go up and down. If it is too loose, the window will fly up and won't stay where you want it. If the rope won't slide behind the sash to the weight opening, you'll have to pry off the front sash. This only takes a few more minutes.

You may also have to glaze some windows in this new career of yours. Sometimes the glaze on a window becomes brittle and falls out around the panes. To correct this, you will need a good glazing compound and a special glazing tool—you can purchase these at your neighborhood hardware store. On windows, determination, persistence, and practice makes perfect, or close to it.

Appliances

If you need new appliances for your home, remember that you can shop for appliances in the classified ads too. There are some great buys to be found there. We've found lovely stoves and refrigerators for a fraction of the cost of new ones, and in the colors we wanted too! Call up and shop for these as you would a house. What color is the refrigerator? Is it in good condition? Can you deliver it? Take a look at it if it sounds like what you are looking for. Then make an offer and negotiate if necessary.

When we're house shopping we frequently ask the owners what they intend to do with their appliances once they move out, whether we're interested in the house or not. Often they intend to sell them, so we tell them we're interested. They have an instant sale, and we find a good buy.

Do you have a husband, relative, or friend who owns a truck? Does this person have an appliance dolly too? We have access to both of these, and can always borrow them for a couple of hours. When you're moving your appliances, be sure to remove all of the parts that might fall off and put them in a secure place.

When we buy homes that will bring in rents of $550–650, we provide our tenants with appliances like dishwashers and garbage disposals. Many investors will advise against this, saying that with fewer appliances, fewer things can go wrong. But with the rent people are paying for the homes, and considering the neighborhoods they're in, we feel we should include these conveniences. When we install a new disposal, we purchase it at a lumber-hardware discount store. It compares in quality to the low-to-middle end of a name brand and is about thirty dollars cheaper. Dishwashers you can find through the wants ads or in department stores.

Kitchens and Bathrooms

If the kitchen and bathrooms on a property really look sad, you may be able to increase the value and rental marketability of your home by putting in new ones. Don't let the thought of this overwhelm you—it's not that expensive. For one property we needed a brand-new bathroom. There wasn't even a subfloor in it! So we literally started from the ground up. We put in a new subfloor, a new toilet, and a new sink. We put up some nice wallpaper too. Does all of this sound incredibly expensive? It wasn't. We bought new toilets and sinks from a building supply center—they run about thirty dollars apiece. (Do not buy these from a plumber; he will charge you quite a bit more.) These facilities are not that difficult to put in. You must be careful with them, though, as the porcelain can break easily. A how-to book will tell you what you need to know; all you have to do is remain confident and calm, and read the instructions carefully.

It's not difficult to fix up a kitchen. If the cabinets are in bad shape, remove them. You'll find that a trusty crowbar will help you do this. You can buy new cupboards and install them yourself or have them installed for you.

Old kitchen cabinets can be altered in several different ways. One method is to remove the doors and drawers. Paint the wall units a neutral color, such as tan or off-white (try to match colors from your kitchen floor or wallpaper). Paint the drawer and doors another bright color from your wallpaper or floor pattern; navy blue, for example, looks great. New hardware from your discount store can do wonders. There are companies that specialize in new cabinet doors and drawer fronts. This saves a great deal of money compared to replacing cabinets altogether. A third trick is to remove an upper cabinet door (or two) which may be in bad repair. Clean the remaining wall units, sand, and fill holes with wood filler. Paint the cabinets, and after your paint dries, wallpaper the back walls of your cabinets with a bright wallpaper. The same pattern you use in the kitchen will work well. Leave the doors off completely. This is inexpensive and attractive as well.

We've found that a quick way to spiff up a kitchen is to buy a new stainless steel sink. These are not at all expensive—with the faucet, they run about thirty dollars. They are easy to put in (just make sure you buy the right size!) and add a great deal to a home. Butcher block counter tops are amazingly inexpensive from a discount lumber store. They also make a big difference.

For cleaning bathroom tile you may find that muriatic acid (a type of hydrochloric acid) is helpful. This is very potent stuff, but it will sure get the job done. Wear gloves and protect your eyes. Make sure the gloves have no holes in them. Dilute the acid with water and spray it on the tile. It will eat up any problems you may have.

Regrouting the tile around the tub is not a difficult task, if you have the proper tools. It really spruces up a bathroom too, and remember what members of our own sex are looking for in a home! Wouldn't *you* like a nice bathtub with clean tiles and grouting? Little additions like this can sway a looker to take your property, whether it's for rent or for sale.

Plumbing

You should not allow all plumbing problems to send you running to the telephone in search of help; there are many jobs you're quite capable of doing. Why call a Master Plumber to repair a leaky faucet? Simply replace the washer. We can tell you how to do this in a few sentences—it's that simple. First, turn off the water for that faucet. Then remove the tops of the handles by snapping off the *H* or *C* with a screwdriver. Now, remove the screw underneath them and the handle will just pull off (unless it has been on for a long time and has corroded, in which case, pry it off). Next, unscrew and remove the stem and replace the washer on the bottom of the stem. Now put it all back together the way you took it apart. Bingo! No leaky faucet.

If the drain trap under the sink springs a leak, you can replace this yourself with the right tools for under eight dollars. The right tools consist of a pair of plumber's wrenches—you'll need one to hold and one to turn. Any how-to book will tell you how to do almost any minor plumbing job. Replacing a drain trap and mending a leaky faucet are both minor jobs. Purchase a handbook on plumbing and heating repairs and choose which jobs you'll do yourself and which you'll contract. The three of us are not as speedy as a professional, but when we're finished it works, and we've saved many dollars doing the work ourselves.

Electrical

Aside from easy jobs like replacing switches and outlet plugs, we decided long ago to leave electrical jobs to a professional. A how-to book is just not enough of a guarantee that we won't electrocute ourselves. None of us have any real desire to learn about electricity anyway . . . and possibly get fried. Ask a city inspector for a recommendation. The inspector will undoubtedly know a good electrician, and the work will pass inspection.

Tools of the Trade

You will find your rehabs much easier if you start collecting your tools *now* and keep them organized. Ninety percent of our time on the first rehab was spent running around looking for the right tools. Since there are three of us and seven children, we have learned to label all our tools with colored tape, and we keep them together in lightweight-plastic tool boxes (we each have one). When we arrive for a project, we're armed with tools, ladders, saws, drills, and gloves (two pairs apiece—for indoors and outdoors. We certainly don't want to touch all that filth, or worse, break a fingernail).

As for tools in your tool box, you'll want screwdrivers (both regular and Phillips, in several sizes), pliers, wrenches, a hammer, knife, putty knife, a measuring tape, razor blades, scissors—anything that makes your work easier. For your plumbing repairs, you'll need a tubing cutter, basin wrench, vice grips, and channel grips. You'll also need to buy some how-to books. You may want to carry these around with you too.

We have one tool we refer to as the Magic Bar. We keep it with our tools and take it everywhere. The Magic Bar is simply a curved crowbar which aids us in everything from removing kitchen cabinets to prying nails out of the floor that are too close to the wall to get at with a hammer. We use the Magic Bar to pry open painted windows and remove tile from kitchen floors. You'll never know when you'll need a tool that will do it all for you, so keep your eyes open for a magic bar of your own.

We also have a large shop vacuum we use on our properties, and a cordless, reversible drill—a Christmas present from our husbands one year, and we were worried that they wouldn't approve of our new careers! We also have a hydraulic jack to level porches.

Remember that all rehabilitation expenses are tax deductible, whether you buy a container of glue or a paint sprayer, so keep all your receipts.

Most of our tools have come from Carol's husband—he loves to collect specialty gadgets that make jobs easier to complete in a short time. He's helped us gather the proper tools for the proper jobs, and is always there when we use our most expensive tool: an airless paint sprayer. This sprayer has paid for itself twice over already. Carol mans the gun and Jane holds the ladder and sprayer. This way, we can spray an entire house in less than a day. But for some reason, we're unable to remember the steps for operating this miraculous tool, and the presence of Carol's husband gives us confidence. If you can find some person who's handy with all types of tools, use his or her services and knowledge as much as possible. These friends are a real treasure.

Contracted Labor

If you do not want to do the work yourself, you should look for a handyman (or woman!) to help you out. Shop for his services as you would anything else. You may want to put an ad in the paper and interview several people. Check references—know what kind of work the handyman has done before.

When you contract to have big jobs done, take several bids to find out competitive rates. Look at some of your handyman's previous work. Whom has he worked for in the past? Make sure he hasn't done work just for his relatives. Is he insured? This is very important—a professional will always be insured. In your written agreement with him, put in a clause that states that you are not responsible for any negligence on his part. It's a good idea to owe him a portion of his money until the job is satisfactorily finished, otherwise he may not be willing to stick around until you're satisfied. Have a signed, written agreement as to the job he'll do and the amount he'll be paid. We always include a bonus if the job is done well and finished earlier than agreed upon, and we deduct some of his pay if it's not finished on time. We let the handyman know that this is our practice. Once the job is finished and your contractor paid, have him sign a release of all liens for that job. We had a stamp made up that we use on the back of our checks that releases all liens when he endorses the check.

By keeping everything written down and having releases, you'll prevent cost overruns.

If you're having work done for you on a property, make sure to be there while the work is being done. We've had some unpleasant experiences when leaving a workman alone on a property. In some cases if no one is watching, he won't work hard. You do not necessarily need to be there the entire day, but make certain he knows you'll be checking on him frequently.

Also be wary if someone is offering to do a job for a very low price. Not too long ago we were taking bids to have about 2,000 square feet of ceiling sprayed. We received one bid that was far below the others, and he said he could start immediately. We couldn't resist it—we hired him.

When we returned to our duplex a couple of days later, we found out why his bid had been so low. The ceilings had not been repaired underneath and he'd sprayed right over the cracks. He had not protected the rest of the room with any coverings; the walls, windows, and floors were covered with about as much white spray paint as the ceiling. We learned our lesson the hard way, and resolved as we scraped paint to be more cautious of incredibly low bids on big projects.

Spraying ceilings should be one of your first jobs. It does cause a mess. After scraping and sanding to get all of that white spray off the walls, windows, intricate woodwork, and floors, we made a discovery: it wipes off with water! We hope you can learn from some of our mistakes. We have made mistakes, but because there are three of us, it is easier to laugh about them and resolve to do better the next time.

Someday we'd like to contract out all of our rehab work because it is very time consuming. We would rather spend our time buying more properties. We do have much more of our work done by handymen now. Ask around to find a reputable person—try your paint store, other investors, friends, etc. We have had very good luck with elderly men. They do fine work and have quite a bit of knowledge they're willing to share with us. They are interested in what we're doing and will offer valuable advice—and they're prompt, a great plus. Once we find such a jewel, we stick with him.

Our handymen are usually happy to work with us. One of the reasons for this is that we pay them on time. For large projects we pay weekly, and if their work requires a large outlay of cash, we have them put the cost of materials on one of our accounts (at a hardware store). We never ask them to spend their own money on our projects. Treat your workmen well. You cannot expect them to work promptly and efficiently if you're not treating them as professionals.

You will probably notice something about some of your handymen: they'll start out at a certain rate for a certain job and that rate will steadily creep up. Before you know it, you will be paying him more than you pay others for the same work! Watch out and don't get taken advantage of.

Once you do a couple of rehabs, all this will seem easier to you. You'll have an idea of how much any job costs and you won't be taken for a ride unless you want to go somewhere. Remember to write everything down, and keep learning from your experiences.

All of your rehabs will not be expensive. Some will take some cleaning, and that's it. Other properties will cost thousands of dollars. Whether you have allotted eight dollars or $8,000 for your rehab, we recommend that you exercise great care in spending your money. When spending a great deal on a rehab, you tend to be more wasteful. Be aware of this tendency and keep on top of it; there's no sense tossing money away.

When you've spent the money you have budgeted for a project, it's time to stop. Do not go any further with it. Yes, the house would likely look just a tad better with some kitchen carpeting, but if you've used up your money, consider your rehab finished. You have already done the important redecorating work, now let the property be. We always follow this rule, or we would be working on a home forever and put far too much money into it. If you feel you must make a showcase of a home, do it with your own.

Your last job on any house is to take pictures of it—pictures of your "new" house. You have done a marvelous job with it. You've just made your home far more marketable; the other landlords and rental property owners in your area are probably green with envy. They also are a bit concerned—your lovely property is going to offer stiff competition for them. But this is what free enterprise should be about: those who work harder reap greater rewards. Congratulations.

You're not finished rehabilitating yet. The last thing we do when our project is complete is to rehab ourselves! We take a day off for manicures, facials, and haircuts. We may even go out shopping for a new outfit. Rehabing leads to a hearty appetite and a sloppy appearance! We always take some time to relax and get back in style when our work is done. It's a great reward.

CHAPTER TEN

Likeable Landlording

YOU'VE ALL HEARD the melodrama about poor little Nell and her run-in with the terrible landlord. We don't enjoy being hissed at, so here are a few tips to make landlording more likeable.

Many people are nervous about the idea of being a landlord. Landlording is a job that makes those interested in real estate shudder—sometimes people use their dislike of this occupation to explain why they don't pursue real estate investments. They complain about tenants, maintenance, late payments, and burdensome responsibilities, thereby adding to the landlord's already sullied reputation. The mere word *landlord* conjures up bad images: pictures of serfs working hard for a laughing master.

Granted, there is a certain type of tenant who can make landlording a headache, but, believe it or not, we don't mind being landlords. We do not have many tenant problems—it is an unusual event when we do. The main reason things go smoothly for us is that we follow some strict guidelines with all of our renters and constantly keep a firm, positive attitude. We think that you'll be able to get along with your tenants, too, if you follow similar guidelines.

We are good landlords. We treat our tenants well and this is usually reflected in their attitude toward us. The three of us learned a phrase when we were teaching, concerning how to approach our students: fair and friendly, but firm. This may sound rather silly, but if you approach your business in this same manner, you find fewer problems. There are landlords who treat their tenants harshly, and they are almost always the ones who have problems with their renters.

135

These landlords cannot keep their homes or units filled, and every time the slightest problem in a rental creeps up, the irate tenant is on the phone, demanding that something be done. At the other extreme, the landlord who is not firm with his tenants will soon regret his lax attitude. Some of his tenants will take advantage of his easy-going attitude, and his rent payments will start coming in late.

If you have problems with your rent payments coming in on time, regardless of the reason, you are placed in a bad position. Lenders are never easy-going about money owed them, and they'll expect you to have your mortgage payments in on time. Can you see why it would behoove you to adopt the "fair, friendly, but firm" attitude as a landlord? Just as with a student and his teacher, a tenant will appreciate a landlord's friendly and fair attitude and will respect her firm approach. By firm we mean, for example, that we're not afraid of saying our rents are due on the first. On the fifth, you will owe an extra twenty-five dollars in late charges. On the tenth you will receive an eviction notice and we will file with our courthouse. We also mean that when a tenant calls to say that he has spent $150 on yard work and would like to deduct this from his rent, we say absolutely not. Repairs must be pre-authorized by us, and we hire needed maintenance.

There are some advantages in being a woman landlord. You will find, as a woman, that your male tenants will do more of their own maintenance on your properties. The reason for this is obvious enough: men feel slightly embarrassed to have to ask a woman to do a repair for them that they could do themselves. Our society has roles for the sexes that can be frustrating, but in this case, ladies, let men play out their role of handyman to the utmost. They can fix a washer on a sink almost as well as we can, so we allow them to do it. Of course, if they do ask us to do some maintenance, we do it or hire someone to fix the problem. But if the egos of our male tenants will make them uncomfortable if they do not rescreen their own window, far be it from us to insist on doing it for them.

We make it a practice to rehabilitate and maintain our investments properly. This way, problems that require us to make a trip to a home are less frequent. If you adhere to this policy, you will probably get the same happy results.

Your rental home or units are ready to go. You have cleaned everything, done some redecorating, and put in the necessary appliances. Your investment property is ready to be leased out to the perfect tenant.

Leasing a property is usually not a difficult process. It only becomes difficult if you try to rent a property for more than the price of the other rentals in the area. You do not want to price a rental too high—this could leave you with an extra payment because you cannot rent the property as quickly. This is why we have stressed repeatedly the importance of researching any area in which you plan to purchase. If you buy a home in an area without knowing what properties are renting for, you might structure your terms blindly, a move that would leave you with homes or units on your hands which will decrease or eliminate your positive cash flow. It takes very little to learn about the rental market in any area. Call your realtor or an agent in the area; call on rental ads yourself and ask questions. Do not guess at rental markets. Always know your area before buying!

Find out about the laws in your state concerning rentals and landlords. Every state has different rental regulations, and as an investor and landlord, you are expected to know them. Become familiar enough with your lease so that you can go through it effectively with your tenant. Decide what sort of lease you are going to offer your tenants—you could offer a month-to-month lease, a six-month lease, or a twelve-month lease. The length of lease you offer depends on the length of time you feel most comfortable with. If you're in a crowded college town where rentals are snapped up in a hurry, you can easily rent your property by the entire year, thereby avoiding any vacancy problems. In some areas, though, the rental market is more competitive and six-month leases draw in more tenants. We prefer a month-to-month lease because we can terminate the lease if the tenant is not adhering to its terms. But you must be careful. Your goal is a long-term tenant, but you will receive many calls from renters who are only interested in a two-month lease.

In Search of the Perfect Tenant

There aren't many perfect tenants out there, but you want to make it your goal to find as many of them as you possibly can. Your first step in finding a good tenant is to put an ad in the paper. This ad, obviously enough, should explain why a renter should want to move into your property. If you can think of any catchy words, by all means use them. You should also give an idea of what your rental is like: how many bedrooms, square footage, whether there's a garage, etc. You haven't too much room in the ad, so point out the most desirable features of your rental in this small space. Whether you advertise the rent payments is up to you—if it's a desirable feature of your rental, you probably should. The more information you include in your ad, the fewer calls you'll receive from tenants who can't afford your property.

A sign including your phone number needs to be placed in the front window or yard of your property. If your property is on a quiet street, find the nearest busy street and put a sign up there too. You can either make your own sign (we talk about this in the chapter on selling your property) or buy a generic one in a hardware or business-supply store. Remember, appearances are important.

If your phone does not begin ringing off the hook, don't be alarmed. When we first began renting and selling, we expected many calls. When they didn't come, we became nervous. If you have put a reasonable rent payment on your property and you did your shopping carefully, your telephone will ring.

Once those calls start to come in, you need to get as much information as you can over the telephone about a prospective renter. By doing this, you can save both your time and the renter's time. You need to know if the rent payment is something the renter can handle. Is this person working? If not, is there a spouse or somebody else who is? If a person is not working, he may have a very difficult time paying his rent promptly. You may want to ask the caller what he's looking for in a rental. This may shock him—many landlords or apartment managers taking rental calls are anything but concerned about the renter's needs. Give him time to catch his breath, and then listen to what he has to say. In this conversation, you will have set a nice precedent of concern for this person's needs. This is a good foundation on which to build a mutually beneficial business relationship, should he go on to become a tenant in one of your properties. If, after hearing his rental needs, you find that you cannot meet them, you can politely hang up.

Try to gauge whether the caller is really interested in seeing your property. If he is, and you have accumulated all the information you possibly can over the phone, set up an appointment. This can be a tricky task. Many people see nothing wrong with not showing up for appointments to see a rental property. Your time has been wasted when this happens—something you want to avoid. We've learned a few techniques through our experience with no shows that we'll share with you.

If you talk to someone on the phone and he's interested in seeing your property, don't allow his enthusiasm to wane. Make the appointment for a time as soon as possible—we always try to make it thirty minutes from the time of the call. Even two hours is enough to allow a person to decide he has better things to do than look at a rental property, and he may not meet you. If the prospective renter simply cannot make an appointment in a half hour, tell him to call you back if he really wants to see the home and you'll arrange something then. Take his number so you can call him back if he can't call you. If the appointment is for the next day or later, make certain your prospective renter calls you, or you call him to confirm the appointment. Explain that you live a long way from the property and that you will not meet him unless he gives you some confirmation that he'll indeed be there.

Set your appointment at a time not on the hour or half-hour. For some reason people don't take appointments at these times as seriously as they do appointments set for 2:10 or 3:35. Who knows why people tend to act this way? Perhaps it's because airlines sometimes set their departure times at odd minutes (though we're on time far more frequently than planes are). Whatever the reason, you will have better luck with your tenants-to-be if you set your appointments at unusual times.

We also make certain that this person knows we're not going to wait for hours. We usually say something like: "It's 4:35 now. I drive a blue car and I'll be there at 5:10—I'll wait for you for ten minutes. At 5:20, if you're not there, I'll leave." This way, callers know that we're busy people and they won't stop for a quick shopping trip on the way.

All three of us live about thirty minutes from most of our investment properties. To drive that distance to show a home to someone who chooses not to come is irritating, a waste of time, and it makes us feel negative about humanity in general. You have noticed by now that we do not enjoy negative situations. We avoid discouragement when it comes to rental property showings as much as possible by trying to make certain that people show up. In spite of our efforts, no shows do occur. You'll be frustrated by them, too, sooner or later—whether you own four properties or forty. There will always be irresponsible people in the world, and you'll just have to deal with them. You wouldn't want such inconsiderate people for your tenants anyway.

When you go to meet your prospective tenant, take the keys to the property, the rental applications, some business cards (you carry these with you all the time, don't you?), and a couple of leases. You may want to simply keep these items in your car in a briefcase or large envelope. We always leave a lease on the property in a kitchen drawer so that we are prepared for anything.

Try to look nice when you see your tenant. Funny as it seems, a tenant will take you more seriously if you look professional in a suit, dress, or nice pants. A woman in blue jeans needs her rent payments paid on time just as much as a woman in a nice suit and heels, but renters sometimes don't appear to think so.

After you arrive at the property and greet the interested rental shopper, show him around, pointing out what a lovely place this would be to live in. Modestly tell this person, as he or she compliments the cleanliness and decor in comparison to the other places he has seen, that you did all the work yourself. Let him know that you own the property and care for it yourself so that he is impressed and thinks you must be a conscientious owner and landlord. You have built a relationship with this renter-to-be—perhaps because you care about what he needs from a rental and he sees this. He likes your property; he likes you and he decides that he wants to move into your rental instead of one of the countless other rentals he has seen. You hand him an application, and he begins to fill it out. The person who readily fills out all the blanks on the application form with checking account numbers, savings account, etc., is usually a qualified renter. Please do not rely on your own judgment, however—run a credit check. We have found, too, that the person who takes an application with him, saying he will get it back to you, usually won't.

A clean, well-kept rental and a pleasant attitude on your part will start the two of you off on the right foot. You tend to attract nicer people when you care for your properties diligently, and your property values will go up. Always maintain and improve your rental properties. You can also ask for a slightly higher rent payment if you are offering quality shelter. Appliances such as a dishwasher and a disposal allow you to up the rent even more—keep this in mind. People who have a disposal, stove, and a dishwasher in the unit they're renting can expect to pay approximately $650 per month for a $70,000 property in our area. This varies greatly throughout the country.

Once the tenant has filled out his application, tell him you'll get back to him after you've checked out his application. Tell him he can move into the unit if, after looking over his application, you are assured that he is a qualified tenant.

Now, using the information that he has supplied on the application, you want to find out as much as you can about your tenant. Your town may even have a renter-screening service that will supply you with application forms. On this application, you should ask for the prospective tenant's full name, his present address, birthdate, social security number, driver's license number, credit information, employer and personal references. You need to know where he used to live and his former landlord's name—also ask what his former rent payments were. It is a good idea to have an emergency telephone number from him too. You may also want to know in writing if he has any pets he wants to bring onto the property. People with pets are always the first to assume that those animals never come inside, but winter in our area can bring sub-zero temperatures and all pets are brought into homes for protection. We chuckle at these people who claim only outside pets.

If you belong to a credit bureau, give it a call and see if there's any information about this individual. The credit bureau should provide you with all the data available, good or bad, and will also have forms to help you record the information they give you. This is why you ask your prospective tenant for credit information, social security number, full name, and former addresses.

If you decide to do a credit check yourself, call this person's previous landlord. Ask the address of his rental property and ask what the rent was per month. This is why you asked for this information on the application—by calling the landlord you are only verifying what you have been told. Many prospective tenants know that former landlords will have nothing nice to say about them, and to avoid being rejected because of their report, they give a friend's name and phone number—but a friend is not likely to know the exact address of the place or the rent paid, so that strategy will often fall through.

You should know that you do not have to do this qualifying process yourself—you could go through a rental screening service. Such a company will run a check on your hopeful tenant within twenty-four hours. Our screening agency provides several services. One is verification of the information acquired, another is a credit check. There is a fee for each of the services. If you would rather not do this necessary task yourself, it will certainly be worthwhile if you were to get someone else to do it for you. We used this screening company at first, until we felt comfortable with the verification process and joined a credit bureau.

Do not trust your assessment of a person on his appearance alone. There is much to be said for woman's intuition, but it can let you down. Your intuition may tell you a person is good-hearted, but it may not specify whether this individual will prove a good renter; he might be so very generous and loving that he invites all of his friends over to stay at his new place for free. And remember that there is no requirement that a good-hearted person must also be a qualified, responsible, tidy person.

We once showed a rental to a lovely couple we were very excited about. They were very warm, friendly, and we thought they would certainly be great renters. We didn't feel it really necessary, but as it's our firm policy to check on every prospective tenant, we went ahead and did a credit inquiry. We called up their former landlord and heard a tale that made us really laugh at ourselves. Yes, this couple was nice enough, but they belonged to a motorcycle group of about twenty members and frequently had all their biking buddies over for tea—

motorcycles were constantly strewn about the residence. They had four children and four ferrets and none of these darling creatures was fully housebroken. They had even received seven eviction notices. We turned this couple down before they could pursue their chosen life-style at our expense. That first impression was a real loser! Are we ever relieved we followed our policy closely.

Always check on prospective tenants, no matter how friendly and trustworthy they appear. You want to see a good background on them, or at least a not very bad one. And make your inquiries before they move in, not after. Always take a security deposit and one month's rent before your tenants move in. Once your tenants are in place, with all of their furniture and a lease signed, it will be at least a month before you can get them out. The applicants will get that month's shelter for free, and you will lose because you failed to make certain they were qualified.

It is not a good idea to mix tenants. If you have decided that you would like to fill your four-plex with elderly people, do not make the mistake of slipping in one twenty-two-year old. You are setting yourself up for problems if you do this. The twenty-two-year old feels he or she has the right to have fun and a right to his personal freedom, but his elderly neighbors may not think along the same lines. When the young tenant has a party until two in the morning, or has members of the opposite sex over at night who don't go home, bad feelings may be created. This type of occurrence makes the gossip start flying. Don't give them anything to gossip about—put younger people in one complex and older ones in another. If an elderly person is very young at heart, and swears he doesn't mind loud music and parties, he could live in a complex with a younger group, but make certain he knows what he's getting into.

If you're pleased with the renter's application after your thorough check on him, call him and set a time to go through the lease together and take his deposit and first month's rent. Be prompt. If you have a lengthy period between accepting the application and notifying him of his acceptance, he may have found another place to live.

Leases

Your lease is a very important document. It clarifies for both you and your tenant what will take place on your property and what the responsibilities of both parties are. Where do you find your leases? Once again, your business supply or stationery shop will be able to help you. There may also be a landlord's organization in your community where a lease can be acquired. If you don't wish to use one of these forms, you can have a lawyer draw one up for you. This is what we chose to do. Our lease is lengthy and covers many items, but we want the tenant to know his rights and we want our rights clarified. In our lease we specify that the tenant must maintain the property (in our rental homes, not our complexes). The lawn is to be mowed, the bushes trimmed, the sidewalks kept free of snow, etc. We do not ignore the inside either—the tenant is to change the furnace filters and pay attention to the air conditioning unit to see that it does not become clogged with debris that might cause problems. If you have any particular requests of the tenant, these should be in the contract too. If, for example, you do not want to see automotive parts on the driveway, specify this in your lease.

Include with your lease a checklist of all the items that your tenant should notice upon moving into your property. How does the carpeting look? Are there any holes in the walls? Do any walls need repainting? Make certain he goes through the property and does this, then mails a copy to you within three days of moving in. Your tenant should understand that any damage found when he wants to move out will be his responsibility if it's not on the list of previous damages. You will take this money from his deposit. We have a checklist we send when we receive notice from a tenant. Also make certain your tenant understands that if he moves out without giving you proper notice, he revokes his right to the deposit money.

Put your pet policy into your lease. Puppies, especially, can be destructive. If you do not want dogs soiling your carpet, state that dogs are not allowed. If you don't mind a cat, specify that one cat (or whatever number you feel is reasonable) is okay, not twenty-seven. You also could say that you allow no pets in your rental, period. But keep in mind that many prospective tenants will deliberately seek out a house rather than an apartment because a landlord of a rental house is more likely to accept animals. You may have a larger market if you allow animals. But remember that pets can do a great deal of damage. We use a pet rider with our house and charge a larger deposit.

A lease should inform the tenant of his rights as far as subletting the property. Will you allow him to do this? In college towns, students are grateful for a subletting right because it gives them an opportunity to find someone else to make their rent payments if they're to leave for the summer. But allowing a tenant to sublet takes some of your control away—you never know who your tenant will put in unless you qualify the new tenant as well. Use your own judgment on this.

Also, spell out in the lease how many people may occupy the unit. A three-

143

bedroom house does not accomodate twenty people for long without showing some extra wear and tear. If you want only one family of four or five in your unit, have it in writing.

Include in your lease the tenant's expectations if he decides to move. Decide on the notice you want (you need to start advertising) and whether you would like to reserve the right to show the property to a prospective tenant or buyer while the tenant is still occupying the property. We have a list of things that must be done before we'll return the tenant's deposit. We ask that the carpets be clean, the windows washed, the back porch swept, the basement and linen closets cleaned out, etc. If any of these tasks are not performed, we have the right to withhold part of the deposit money in order to have the tasks done once the person has moved out. The amount that each task is worth is written into the lease so the tenant can see if cleaning out the garage is worth his while. If you draw up your own lease, make sure it follows the laws of your state. This will be vital if you have to go to court.

In the lease, inform the tenant when the rent is due and the length of the lease. It is best to make the rents from all of your tenants due on the same day, preferably the first of the month. It is much easier to keep track of who has paid and who has not with this method. If someone moves in after the first, prorate the rent for that first day of a month and then get your tenant on a regular first-of-the-month billing schedule. Our late charges are also spelled out in our lease, and so are our "insufficient funds checks" charges. (You may have a few of these too.)

As a landlord, you'll hear every story imaginable from your tenants as to why the rent is late or the check bounced. Do not accept this as reason for them not to pay their late fee or returned-check charges. Excuses for unpaid rent range from "I didn't have a stamp," to "My mother in Pittsburgh sprained her ankle," which we recently heard after the tenant had been living in our home for a year. If someone tells you that he was expecting to get some money from his girlfriend after her grandmother's estate was settled—"the old lady just died— I'm so depressed about it"—but it didn't come because of a freak snow storm in Florida, be sympathetic. Explain to him you are very sorry, but you'll need your rent money plus the late charge fee immediately. If you really feel sorry for someone, explain that you, too, have bills to pay and that your lender sympathizes with no one. If lenders will take the farm from broke Aunt Bessie with her seven kids, be assured they'll also take this investment house from you for not paying your bills. Punctual tenants are the key to a successful business. You cannot tolerate any excuses for long. There are those renters who might

144

attempt to take advantage of their female landlords. Nip this tendency before it leads to an eviction. Be firm from the beginning! The longer you delay in getting this month's rent, the less likely next month's rent will be.

If you are given a bad check, be extra firm. In some states it's against the law to write a bad check. Know what your state's policy is, and make sure your tenant is aware of this law. Whether a state puts a fine on rubber checks or not, you should include one on your lease. We charge a ten dollar bounced-check fee on top of the late charge. If you receive a check that has been returned for insufficient funds and a tenant tells you that he wants to make it up as he pulls out his checkbook, tell him that you will accept only cashier's checks for the next couple of months, until he can prove to you once again that he's responsible. You do not want this to happen twice.

We also include in our lease our right to evict someone if he does not pay his rent on time or if he is damaging the property through neglect or abuse. We do not like to have to evict anyone. It is not a pleasant task. If we do have to evict someone, we do not approach the offending tenant alone. There is support in numbers; we go together.

You can buy an eviction notice in that wonderful business supply store of yours, too, or you can have a lawyer help you draw one up. If you have to evict someone, it may be a lengthy and tangled process with some potential emotional storms. You want the advice of a lawyer and/or your local sheriff. Consult your attorney, other investors, or your real estate agent: What is the procedure for evicting a tenant? Your county administration offices can give you more information on this subject. You need to know how to go about serving papers properly and legally or this could really become a long, drawn-out process. In our state you can send this certified mail, but you need to check the laws in your state. Your local courthouse should have the landlord-tenant laws in your area.

This sounds pessimistic. If it makes you feel any better, we have had to evict only one tenant. But it will probably happen to you at least once as you accumulate properties.

Our lease is lengthy and tight, but it gets the results we want. And after going through this lease with us, the tenant is not compelled to sign if he feels we're asking too much from him. That's why we take the time (it will be about thirty minutes before you get through a detailed lease) to explain all of our terms thoroughly.

We have always believed that if a job is worth doing at all, it's worth doing correctly. Remember our saying: Do the right job right. Being a landlord is never easy, but it can be easier if you are on duty from the very beginning.

Good Relations

You should keep very specific records of all correspondence and phone calls with your tenants. If you are concerned about the lack of outdoor maintenance and give a tenant a call, write this down on an activity sheet formulated specifically for this. Any late payments by a renter should be noted, and if you make an inspection of the house, record your impressions of the housekeeping—whatever they are.

This should not be just a negative reporting notebook. If the house looks particularly nice and a tenant always pays his bills on time, record this. Mention it to your tenant: "You're always so prompt with your rent payments. I want you to know that I really appreciate it. You make my job so much easier," or, "You keep up the lawn and the landscaping so nicely. Thank you so much. I really am happy to be working with you." Positive reinforcement always gets results. A tenant is less likely to let his responsibilities slide when he knows the good job he's been doing is recognized.

If we have a particularly good tenant, we don't mind writing a letter to his employer telling him how pleased we are with his employee's responsible attitude. Our tenants are pleasantly surprised by this—such good reports can help win a raise more easily. At Christmas, we make a point of giving our tenants some little gift, letting them know we appreciate their care for our properties and their prompt payments. There is a lot to the saying, "Use a carrot instead of a stick."

The people who live near your property are a valuable resource. Ask them how they think the house is maintained and whether your tenants are good neighbors (no loud parties, trash left out, etc.). We always make it a practice to drive past our properties regularly to make certain they're being maintained. We also use a bi-yearly furnace check as an excuse to go through the home and make certain it is not being abused. You may want to do this also. Your houses are valuable—do not allow them to be neglected.

If a tenant calls you and would like to meet with you about something, and you're working out of an office outside your home, have him meet you there. Don't allow a tenant to come to your own home. In the first place, if your home is nicer than the one that he's renting, he might resent it. And, along with this, you never know how a person will react to the relaxed, non-official situation of a meeting in your home. If he doesn't pay his rent and you're forced to evict him, it could get ugly. He may be a person you don't want knowing where you live.

Always use the considerable diplomatic and persuasive powers that you have developed when working with a tenant. If he's late with the rent money one month, you cannot let it go, but be considerate as you ask him about the delay: "Mr. Jones, I was surprised to find this month that your rent money didn't come in with the others. As you have always paid on time in the past, I'm wondering if there's a problem." He is not going to become defensive with this approach, but he probably would become a bit upset if you simply demand, "Where's the money?"

If you're talking with an individual who wanted to move into one of your properties but you've found that his credit rating or background make him an unacceptable candidate, buffer the rejection a bit. " Mr. Smith, there are some very good things on your credit rating, but you seem to have had a problem here. . . . " Who knows? Maybe that problem was a credit rating myth that should have been on another Mr. Smith's report. Give people a chance to talk— they might be able to explain themselves. Do not be mushy or easily swayed by their explanations, but if they have a valid reason for something in their background, you should know what it is. And a person should always know why he or she is being questioned.

Perhaps some of you have heard those notorious stories about calls in the middle of the night about overflowing toilets, exploding water lines, etc. One always hears these horror stories and becomes discouraged about becoming a landlord. Well, let us set the record straight by saying that we have never received a call in the night from an irate tenant who wanted us to get out of our pajamas and into our work clothes. We *have* received calls first thing in the morning, when we were in a position to do something about it other than yawn. Our tenants seem to be aware that most problems are better handled by someone awake, alert, and capable of intelligent response. You may have visions of an exploding water pipe and water cascading all over your tenant's head—perhaps this is your excuse for not becoming a landlord. Such catastrophes do not happen often, and if you properly maintain your houses and screen your tenants, they are not at all probable. As we say (knock on wood), it hasn't happened to us. Don't stay awake too many nights waiting for the phone to ring.

Most tenants are good people and will treat your property well. You do sometimes hear nasty rumors about tenants living in filth on an unknowing investor's property, but this does not happen often. In fact, it's nearly impossible if you check your property often. Because they are unusual, such stories receive attention and people talk about the problems of landlords. Few are interested in hearing how Ms. Smith always pays her bills on time and keeps her rented house so nice, but people will listen if you tell them that five Dobermans killed their owners on your property and it took you six months before you found out. Driving by your properties can save you a great deal of headaches. If your property is going downhill, you can recognize the problem early. Treat your tenants with respect and dignity. If you do, you'll find that success comes more easily to you.

We've talked about many of the negative aspects of being a landlord in this chapter. Honestly, we have had very few problems with our rental properties, simply because we use sound management techniques. Any problems are more than compensated for when we visit our accountant and learn that we're paying no income taxes on this fantastic income we are making because we are landlords.

If you are still hesitant, remember that you can be a property investor and never see your tenants. There are plenty of good management companies out there who would be more than happy to take over these responsibilities for you. You will pay them for their services, but it may be worth the money if managing your units yourself is a problem—for lack of time or because it makes you feel too uncomfortable. We choose to do it ourselves, for now, anyway. We're becoming very busy as we buy more homes—too busy to manage properties, perhaps. Whatever you decide to do, expect the best from your rentals. They should be producing a positive cash flow, providing you with a tax break, and allowing you to have a fascinating career.

We have included several sample forms in Appendix A that you may find useful in your landlording.

PUBLISHER'S NOTE:

One of the most frequently asked questions is "How do I get started?" The publisher has produced a helpful book filled with answers and suggestions about *How To Get Started Investing In Real Estate*, written by Wade B. Cook. Included in this informative 30-page book is why real estate is a good investment area, which angle of investing is best for you, nothing down techniques, how to find good deals, and more.

The publisher will send a free copy of this book upon request. Send your request to:

Regency Books
P.O. Box 27368
Tempe, AZ 85282

Please include $1 to cover postage and handling.

PUBLISHER'S NOTE:

Would you like to have a monthly update on the latest trends and workable ideas for investing in real estate?

Wade Cook's "Inside Real Estate" newsletter is for those of you who would like to keep pace with the most progressive investment experts in the country. It is the country's "what to do," "how to do it," "what's happening" newsletter for the real estate investor who wants to be successful in today's market. Each month there are feature articles covering all aspects of real estate investing, along with other regular sections including tax tips, seminar schedules, and questions and answers. Twelve issues per year.

For a sample copy of "Inside Real Estate," send $5 with your name and mailing address to:

Inside Real Estate
P.O. Box 2-U
Tempe, AZ 85282

CHAPTER ELEVEN

Reaping
the Rewards

WHAT ABOUT SELLING A HOUSE? How in the world do I go about that?

Don't let the idea of selling a house scare you. Selling a home is not difficult, if you know your market and the proper techniques. We have never had any major problems selling our properties, and we have sold a number of them.

Selling your first investment property can give you a wonderful feeling—you are actually reaping the rewards of your time and labor. All that shopping and rehab work seems worth it when you have a check in your hand that allows you a profit of $15,000. This sort of cash certainly makes a trip to London a bit more of a reality, don't you think? You could climb on a plane right now, if you wanted, or take the money and continue building your property investment pyramid.

We normally plan our method of pulling out our profit before we ever make an offer to buy a property. The way that we plan to make our profit has a tremendous impact on the type of offer we make.

There are many ways to profit from a good investment. The method you choose will be determined by your own needs (see Appendix B). Before you buy is the time to consider your income tax benefits. There are many ways to profit without losing your tax benefits. If you are ignoring all the tax breaks available by renting a property, and simply looking for a profit, you may want to turn around and resell the property. This is called, appropriately, a "turnaround sale."

Because one of our many goals is a tax benefit, we usually use one of the methods that lets us enjoy tax savings. We will discuss these first, and then turn our attention to sales.

Lease Option

Our favorite tax-saving method of producing profits is the lease option or the lease purchase sale. We use this approximately seventy-five percent of the time. A lease with an option is the key to the success of our business. It is an excellent technique for many reasons.

In a lease with option, you are simply renting the property to someone who has the goal of owning a home. You are in total control of how you choose to give the option. The option can be for any specified time period you're comfortable with. We have used the period of one year so we could have the benefit of capital gains on our sale. Now, with the change in the tax laws, a six-month option would also allow capital gains benefits.

We normally lease the home for a little above the fair market rent, but we give a portion of the rent toward the down payment if the tenant decides to take the option to buy. We usually take a $1,000 option deposit which will also be credited toward the down payment in the event the home is purchased. We consider this option deposit to be partially a security deposit. If the renter leaves the home and does not buy it, we return the deposit, but only if the home is left in the same condition as the renter found it. The numbers we use can be changed to suit your own needs, and can give you a great deal of control over whether the lessee will actually buy your home or not.

The agreement to lease with an option to buy is simply a page we add to the back of our regular rental agreement. We had this page, as well as our rental agreement, drawn up by an attorney in the area. This option page states that the lessee has the option of purchasing the home for a stated dollar amount within a set period of time. The lessee is required to state his intention in writing at least ninety days prior to the date of the expiration of the option. One advantage of this method is that you do not need to have a vacant property while you're waiting to sell it. Leases with options are terribly popular with young couples, and usually these houses are filled quickly. Not only is someone now making the payments for you, but you also have that option deposit in the bank.

Another advantage of this technique is the caliber of the tenant living in your home. Your tenant cares about the home. He is planning to buy it if he can. He is the type of individual who has the desire to own a home rather than rent one.

Advantage number three is that you have a great deal of control over whether the tenant actually exercises his option or not. The way you structure the option can affect the lessee far more than you realize. If you really would like to own this property and are not particularly eager to sell it, then you may let your tenant put down a small option deposit and put only a very small part of his payment toward the purchase price of the house each month. If you would like to sell, ask for a larger option deposit and give a greater amount of credit each month.

Another benefit is that you are collecting higher rents for the property than you would normally be able to charge. If, for example, the house should rent for $450, we would probably charge $495 per month but give the leasee $100 credit towards the purchase price. If the option is exercised, then this amount is applied to the down payment. If, however, the option is not exercised, then this amount is not refunded and it becomes rent.

Another point to note is that in the majority of cases the option is *not* exercised. Why is this an advantage? Because we are able to collect a larger amount of rent on our property and that extra amount will not have to be refunded. If we use this technique on several of our properties, then our cash flow is much better and we continue to own those properties.

One of the most beneficial aspects of this arrangement is that we are able to sell the property—if the option is exercised—for top dollar. The price that we put on the property for the option price is the top price we would ask for it if we listed it with a real estate company. The only difference is that we don't have to pay a commission.

We have used this technique over and over on almost every piece of property we acquired. As we said, the majority of the time these options are not exercised. This is probably due to the fact that the leasing couple has not been able to save any additional money through the option period, and so lacks the money for the down payment. Or perhaps it's because after living in the house for a year they don't like it as much as they did when they first moved in. Whatever the reason, we really don't care! At the end of a lease option, we've had a good tenant and a very good rent. We either let the lessee stay on at the same rent or we ask him to leave, depending on our intentions for the property and our feelings for him as a tenant. This method has given us a very successful program for all of our properties. We get good rents, all the tax advantages of owning property, and also a few sales at top prices!

Lease Purchase

Another method very similar to this which we use on a property we want to sell is what we call a lease purchase. In this transaction we write a lease agreement and a sales contract at the same time. Instead of calling a deposit "option money," we call it "earnest money." The other party is signing a contract to buy a home. We will also apply a portion of each month's rent to the down payment. The only difference between this and a lease option is that here, the deposit is not refunded should the signer not actually buy it.

We use this technique on a home we've financed with a short term note from a bank or that for some other reason needs to be sold. We may use this method if we want to pull a large profit out of the home after six months or so. Perhaps the area of the property is not appreciating very quickly and we feel it would be better to invest in another area—in that case we generally try to sell the property as quickly as possible. We might feel that our property will actually go down in value if we continue to own it for a long period of time.

When you use this method, you'll want to prequalify your tenant. You need to be sure this tenant can get a loan if he needs one in order to purchase the property. This is when we run a good credit check and help our prospective buyers work out any credit problems they may have.

Refinancing

There are some properties you will want to hang on to. You may want to own this property for your retirement. Perhaps this area is being zoned for commercial purposes and will be more valuable in a few years. How can you pull out some profit and still own the property? There are many ways of doing this, but probably the simplest is to refinance or place a second mortgage on the property. Remember the example we gave of the $50,000 house we bought? We gave the owner $25,000 in cash (borrowed from a bank) and had him carry a second mortgage on our apartments. In essence, we were pulling out the profit from our hard work on our apartments. You could go to a bank and take out a normal second mortgage and then have cash to work with.

Because actually selling a home can be a time-consuming project, and because—as you know—we hate empty properties that are eating up our profits, we use any method we can for selling while someone is living in our home, making payments for us.

154

Selling to Investors

One technique that has proven very easy and allows us the benefits of a renter present in the property, is to sell the property to another investor. If you're trying to sell a home, do not feel timid about letting your fellow investors in your investment group know that you're looking for a buyer. There are many investors out there who are simply looking for the tax savings and appreciation from rental property. They are not in this field as a full-time career in order to make a living, like we are. They would love to find a nice clean property, not in need of anything! They would really love to find out that the property doesn't even need tenants—it comes with a supply of its own, with a very good payment history. Many of our properties were suited for a sale such as this. One example of this would be a property with assumable financing, or one in which we are in a position to do a wrap-around, owner-financed sale with a small down payment. When we do this we make our profit in monthly installments rather than large cash sales. This is much better at income tax time.

Selling Your Property

Only rarely do we ever put a property up for sale. The thing to remember about actually selling your empty house is that there are a number of homes in your city for sale. Buyers have many choices as they look for homes—it's not likely they'll buy something they feel is overpriced. It is a buyer's market right now, so the price you put on your property should be reasonable and the terms should be creative and interesting. You wouldn't buy an overpriced house, and you'll find that few other people would, either.

You have many things to consider when you decide to sell your property. First, you must decide whether you will use a real estate agency or not. You must then decide how you want to get your equity out of the house: in one lump sum, or in monthly payments. If you want your money in one sum, you'll want your buyer to come up with cash. As most people do not have this amount of money sitting around in their piggy banks, your buyer will need to find his financing elsewhere. If you would rather take your money in monthly payments over the next twenty or thirty years, then you should offer owner financing. This is one way to go to pay less in taxes.

You need to consider what kind of terms you're going to offer your buyer. If your loan is assumable, will this be the best alternative for your buyer? Or are you going to have to finance the sale as the owner? What interest rate are you going to offer a buyer if you do finance the sale? Maybe you are considering a combination of these two—letting the buyer assume your mortgage and then financing the rest to get your equity out of the home. Is it possible to "wrap" the existing mortgage? There will be more profit for you if this is possible. Or, are you simply planning to send the buyer to find his own financing? You need to think these things over before you place your ads or go to a realtor.

Using an Agent

The easiest way to sell a home (though not necessarily the quickest) is to go through a real estate agency. Your hard-working realtor will do many things for you that you would otherwise have to do for yourself: He'll do all of the advertising, showings, negotiating,and buyer qualifying, and arrange the closing. A realtor will advertise your property in the local newspapers. Remember that advertising is expensive and your salesman's company will pay for it if you go through an agency. Your real estate agent will also put your house in the Multiple Listing Service books of your city—as an unlicensed seller of property, you cannot do this. Once your home is in an MLS book, all other agents in the area will see that your home is listed for sale and may take a crack at selling it to any buyers who come to them for help in finding a home. With this many people working to sell your home, it may sell faster.

A realtor or his agency will answer all the calls on your home, leaving you free from that responsibility. While your realtor does all this work for you, you could be out looking for more homes to buy. If you use a realtor, you will sign a listing agreement with him for sixty or ninety days. In the agreement, you agree to give this agent the exclusive right to sell your home for the next two or three months. Because of this, it is in your best interest to find an aggressive and hard-working real estate agent. To pay for his services, a realtor will take about seven percent of the price you get for your home. This, of course, will come out of your profits.

Selling Your Own Property

Another way to sell a home is to sell it yourself. This means you do all the showings, negotiating, and paperwork, but you do not pay anyone a commission—all the money you receive for your home is yours to keep once the liens against it and closing costs are paid off.

If we ever do choose to simply sell a home, we like to sell our homes ourselves, even if it's additional work for us. We do this because we can hold on to more of our profits by not paying an agent's commission, and because we've found we can sell a house much faster without him, even though an agent can give our houses more exposure. Before anything happens at all, a realtor has to come out and take a look at our home, settle on an asking price for it, and then put the house into the MLS, all of which takes time. The MLS will then have to take pictures of our home—it will be a couple of weeks before our listing actually comes out in the books. We want our money as quickly as possible, and so we find it difficult to be patient with this lengthy process.

We like the control we have over the sale when we do it ourselves. We like to write our own ads and show the houses—this way we have a better idea of what kind of buyer we're dealing with because we're working directly with him. We enjoy dealing with people and helping them get into a house of their own. It's fun to sell houses—it's all part of the real estate investing process we like so much. For these reasons, we usually skip the services of a realtor when we're ready to sell one of our homes.

If you decide to sell your properties yourself, you'll need to find out some information that a real estate agency normally takes care of for you. For example, you'll need to know the schools children would attend if they moved into your home. You can find out by calling the school district office or asking neighbors with school-age children. Also be able to tell any callers what the child-care situation is in the neighborhood.

You also need to know where the water comes from, what type of sewer services the area has, and what shopping facilities are close. Callers may ask about the zoning of a property—make sure you can tell them what it is. A real estate agent puts all this information on a listing sheet—you'll find yourself much more organized if you do the same. Make up your own listing sheet with all the information anyone could possibly ask about. You may want to keep these listings in a notebook you can thumb through in a hurry if you have several properties for sale at once.

The best place to advertise your house is the newspaper. This is where you check to see what houses are available and where everybody else does too. You've seen the number of ads in your paper—there are literally hundreds in any American big-city newspaper. Since advertising will cost you each day your ad appears, you want it to receive a lot of attention. To do this, you must have something in your ad that makes people look at it twice and think, I should probably give these people a call.

The biggest attraction that a person looking through the real estate ads will notice is creative terms. If you offer owner financing at ten percent for a reasonably-priced home and you advertise this in the paper, you'll receive enough calls to keep you busy. If you want to get some cash out of the home, you'll want to offer some other type of terms, but try to be flexible and open-minded. Make sure your ads reflect your willingness to consider appropriate alternatives to bank-financed mortgages, and your ad will be noticed more quickly.

"For Sale" Signs

One thing you do not want to overlook is the sign you use on the property itself. We're very proud of our own way of taking care of this, because we use our advertising signs as visible examples of our interest in and care of the property. If you're going to sell your house yourself, you're going to need a sign in the yard. A real estate agent will normally hammer in one of his company's signs, but as an owner selling a house yourself, you'll have to buy or make your own. The "For Sale by Owner" signs you see in business supply stores are a valid way to go, but they sometimes tend to look boring. If you're going to be in real estate investing for a while, consider having your own signs made to order for you. You can have these signs designed by someone else or you can do all the work yourself. To have the signs made will be relatively expensive, about forty dollars per sign.

You can probably guess what our reaction was to this. Of course, we made our own signs. We have "For Sale" signs and "For Rent" signs that we designed (with the aid of the graphic artist who also helped with our cards and stationery). We painted and assembled them ourselves. It's not as hard as it sounds! To do this, simply draw a design on a regular 8½ by 11 inch sheet of paper and cut it into four equal pieces. Go to your copy shop and have them enlarge each piece on the color paper you find appealing. Take these four pieces and put them together on a piece of plywood or poster board and glue them down. Then lay some clear contact paper over the design, or laminate it. Voila! Your sign is finished! It's waterproof, it displays the needed information, and it looks much more original and eye-catching than those "For Sale by Owner" signs anybody can buy anywhere.

Your Potential Buyer

When we advertise a property for sale, we also publish the terms of the sale. If we want to pull some cash out of a home immediately, our buyer will need to know that he has to find some form of financing. We have made it our policy to help our prospective buyers find that financing. Before we put a house on the market, we research the loans available by calling loan companies and asking what they have to offer in terms of interest rates and down payments. We find the lowest of these and advertise them in our ads along with what the monthly payment on the home will be. This way, our buyer knows without making a call if he can afford to own our property. We save his time and ours by doing this.

When you receive calls on ads or signs, be courteous to the caller—he could make you some money. Ask him if he feels comfortable with the payments and the down payment you're asking. As we advised you in the chapter on being a landlord, find out as much as possible about the potential buyer over the telephone. See if he is genuinely interested.

When showing the property, be aware of the way you phrase certain sentences. A few choice words can make the difference in whether the prospect chooses to purchase. Use appealing words. We do not use the word *buy*. We always use the word *own*. We say, "Would you like to own your own home?" Remember, owning is fun, buying costs money. Also use the words *initial investment* instead of *down payment*. Again, both expressions may mean exactly the same thing, but one sounds better than the other, and will probably get a more positive response.

Since you're going to be selling quite a few homes in your career, you may want to pick up a book on selling from your bookstore or library.

If you choose to owner-finance your property, you will not be working through a lender or a loan company, so you must take the contract to a title company yourself. The company will handle the sale for you, and the closing can be held more quickly than the six or eight weeks that other forms of financing require. If you are owner-financing your property, it would be beneficial to provide your buyer with an amortization schedule. Call the real estate commission in your state—find out whether a private party is required to provide a disclosure statement if he makes a loan.

Any person signing a real estate contract has three days to back out of it. You should be aware of this—anyone who buys your home has a legal right to cancel the contract within three days.

Qualifying a buyer is much the same process as qualifying a renter. The prospective buyer should give you his full name, social security number, and vital information, and basically the same information you would receive on a rental application.

Belonging to a credit bureau will prove its value when you want to qualify a buyer for your home. Be cautious with your buyers. You want to be sure a buyer is an individual who will make his payments. If he does not, you'll eventually get your house back, but a foreclosure is a long and draining process. You can do your best to avoid that circumstance with a thorough credit check. Talk to the possible buyer's former landlords, his employers, or lenders who have worked with him before. Even if your buyer drives up in a limousine and wears thousand-dollar designer suits, run a check to see if he's qualified.

If your buyer doesn't have a good credit rating, give him some advice as to how to make it better. Be straightforward and honest—that way the two of you part on good terms. That is the only way to run a successful business.

Conventional Lender

If your buyer is going to go through the lender you suggested to get conventional financing, you must draw up a contract on the property for the buyer to take to a loan company. The lender takes over from there. The company officials will handle all of the paperwork, and in six to eight weeks, if your buyer qualifies, you'll be able to collect the check.

If you bought your home with a low interest rate, you may want to do a wraparound when you sell it. As we explained in the financing chapter, a wraparound is a form of owner financing. You hold on to the low interest of your loan and you give the buyer a deed of trust for a higher interest rate or sell the home for a higher price than you paid for it, giving you a monthly check to cover your own mortgage payment. You ask your buyer for a down payment that will cover the down payment you paid. An example will explain this better—get out your mortgage payment schedules book and go through this with us.

Suppose you buy a home through owner financing and the seller was very desperate, so he sold you the home for $43,000 with $3,000 down at an interest rate of nine percent to be paid over a period of twenty-five years. Your payment is $336 (principal and interest) a month to this former owner. After buying the house you turn around and sell it for $59,000—your buyer gives you a $4,000 down payment (which more than covers all the money you have put into the property) and you owner-finance the remaining $55,000 at a higher interest rate for twenty-five years. Your buyer's payments to you are $579 a month. The difference between what your buyer is paying you and what you pay the owner you bought the home from is $243. That money is a positive cash flow, the magic of real estate investing. You have wrapped the mortgage you're giving your buyer around the mortgage the former owner gave you—your new buyer makes payments to you and you have a monthly cash flow after your payment. You also have your $3,000-plus back to go to the marketplace with and do it again. Wraparound sales such as these are wonderful ways to sell your home if you're looking for a good cash flow. They can give you a tax advantage when you sell—you're not taking in a large sum of money all at once. We suggest you read Wade Cook's *How to Build a Real Estate Money Machine* to understand all the advantages of this.

Due-on-Sale Clauses

Due-on-sale clauses are something you have to deal with sooner or later. They can work for or against you. A due-on-sale clause is a clause in a trust deed or a mortgage that will help protect the lender. A due-on-sale clause requires that the holder of a mortgage pay off the mortgage before he resells the home. An owner cannot wrap a mortgage with a due-on-sale clause. His buyer will have to place new financing on the property to purchase the home.

These due-on-sale clauses are included in trust deeds so that the lender will receive all of his money when the house is sold again. A due-on-sale clause in a contract will not allow a buyer to assume a loan. Know what to expect if you have a due-on-sale clause in a trust deed, because it will affect the way you sell your home later.

A seller may include a due-on-sale clause to protect himself if he is owner-financing. Before you put such a clause in one of your contracts, you should know that you can put a clause in any mortgage saying that you have the right to call the loan due or to run your own credit check on the future buyer of your house, and that the resale of that house is contingent upon your approval of the new buyer. This way you are protecting yourself from any new buyers who may purchase the home and be unable to make their payments, but you are not forcing the owner to conform to a due-on-sale clause. You might also include a clause in which a new owner gives up his redemptive rights. Then, if something does go wrong, you can foreclose and get your house back more quickly.

If you have a large loan on your house that can be assumed, it will be a big plus when the time comes to sell. If your loan can be easily assumed, you won't have to wait for the great red-tape machine to qualify your new buyer. By allowing the new buyer to assume your loan, you can either take your equity in cash or you can finance some and take some in cash—it's up to you.

One good way to sell your property quickly, *and* get the cash you want out of it, is to refinance (go to the bank and get a new loan), getting up to eighty percent of the home's value, and then allow the buyer to assume the new loan. This strategy will allow many buyers to purchase your property who would be turned down at the bank but who can afford the monthly payments.

Selling a Vacant Home

You may be tempted to turn off the utilities in a vacant house you are try-ing to sell. Though on the surface that may make sense, it may not be a good idea. Few people will be impressed with the cold, dark house (or the hot, musty, un-air-conditioned house) you show them after abandoning the house to the weather. Most people will also want to turn the lights and the water in a house on and off a couple of times to make sure they won't be facing any surprises. Your house will show much better if it's heated and has water to rush through the pipes for the curious shopper.

Let us cite an example of a small three-bedroom ranch home we purchased for $12,000 below market value. When we looked at the home the realtor informed us it had been on the market for quite some time. The owners had been making payments on two homes. This particular home was in what seemed to be excellent condition, but it needed a good cleaning. The back had a nice family room added on with a corner fireplace. The family room was a very nice addition, but it usually darkens the kitchen when a room is added onto the back, since it removes windows to the outside.

Looking at the home in the late afternoon, we could hardly see the darkened kitchen (the most important room in the house). The seller had turned off the electricity to save a few dollars each month! How much do you think he lost due to that decision? No one likes a dark, cold, dusty kitchen. He accepted our offer of $34,000. We added lighting, put up light wallpaper, cleaned, put the house back on the market (and sold it) for $51,000!

Whether you're leasing or selling a property, there are a few tips on show-ing the home that might be beneficial.

You should arrive ahead of your shopper. Turn on all lights, unlock doors, and make the shopper feel welcome. Little things make a difference, including your own appearance. While it's very tempting to run over to the property in your jeans, we've found that our percentage of sales is exceedingly higher if we're dressed well. The smell of a home is important as well. While some people suggest using vanilla extract sprinkled in the oven, we have found that the scent of your favorite cleaning solution works just as well. Clean windows, clean switch plates, and clean cupboards make an impression too.

To summarize, our rule is to pull the profit out of a property any way we can without letting it sit vacant. Once in a while we do have a turn-around sale, but we know going in that a house will sit empty while it's being sold and we figure this into our expenses. The key to a quick turn-around sale is advertising the terms. Remember, a turn-around sale does not allow the benefits of capital gains taxation on your profit. A wraparound sale or a lease option are better when considering taxation benefits and long-term cash flow.

CHAPTER TWELVE

Keep Going! (Perseverance)

THREE AND A HALF years ago, three young mothers in their youngish thirties decided to embark on an exciting adventure. To understand how we have managed to turn from elementary school teaching to real estate investing, living by our brawn *and* brain, we need to take you back a few years.

When Lynda thinks back ten years, to when her oldest son was still a baby, it is not with fondness and nostalgia. She was baby-sitting two small children in her home to make ends meet. Talk about being tied down! Day after day, wrist deep in diapers, fixing peanut butter sandwiches and refereeing babies . . . she could feel her mind slowly atrophy and she watched helplessly as her dreams began to die.

She recalls sitting on the kitchen floor, telephone in one hand and baby in the other, talking to her friend Jane. Jane, too, was feeling trapped by small children and a bleak existence. They talked idly about finding some way to exercise their minds and bodies . . . maybe they could buy a small house and fix it up. They could even take the children with them to help. But where would they get a down payment? So they dropped the idea . . . for a while.

Carol, after a year of marriage, purchased her first home with her husband. He was afraid that she was nailing him down to earth permanently, but Carol really only wanted to fix up their home and move on in a couple of years. She found, however, that her conservative husband was not agreeable to change, and her plans were out of the question.

It was twelve years and two daughters later before she saw the inside of her next home. At that time she told her realtor friend to please help her find a way to buy her new home and keep her old fixed-up home as a rental. She had a 5¼ percent VA loan with a $125 monthly payment and only a $10,000 balance that would be paid off in ten years. She knew how much rent the house would bring in, and the home was in excellent condition. The answer her realtor gave her was, "Carol, you don't want a rental. They're a pain in the neck." She took him at his word, and her desire to invest was squelched, for a while.

By this time Lynda was divorced and back in school, teaching. Life wasn't all roses on an $800 a month income. But her passion for decorating hadn't waned, and she still spent her leisure hours looking through model homes and flipping through wallpaper books.

Jane hadn't lost her interest either. She was sure she could fix up any home, and she was still looking for an investment home to buy. During one summer vacation she read everything she could find in the local library on real estate investing. The books were outdated and the prices quoted were a fraction of current prices. She decided that investing in real estate might have worked at one time, but it was simply too late for her.

Perhaps it was a stroke of luck that brought us together one special evening for the introductory portion of an investment seminar. All of the old dreams were rekindled, and throwing caution to the wind, we pulled out our charge cards and paid for the remainder of the seminar the American way—with plastic. After years of schooling, on both sides of the desk, we took the most exciting course of our lives.

Every successful woman started out slowly. Geraldine Ferraro wasn't nominated for Vice President of the United States the day she graduated from law school, and Gloria Vanderbilt wasn't a household name when she began designing clothes. None of the rich and famous women (and men) we three admire made it in one day, and few in one year. The wheels slowly turned, and finally they were rolling headlong into success.

So it was with us. At first we moved slowly and cautiously, considering each decision carefully, until we gradually became at ease with the business and investment world. Compare us with the tortoise, from the tortoise and hare fable. We worked slowly, building success upon success. We didn't make our first million in our first year, but we didn't make any major mistakes, either.

The first year as investors we purchased only six properties, the second year we purchased twelve properties, and the third year it was even more. Now we're rolling along at the rate of four every month. Patience, persistence, and a daily commitment to success—if you have dreams, there is no other way.

We could have quit teaching long before we actually did—we probably could have quit the day we bought our first home, and we would have survived the decision. But we wanted to be sure we were going into the right field, that we liked what we were doing, and that we could make a living at it. We want you to feel secure with your career change decision too.

We told you about the series of properties we worked on over a period of a couple of months—we deposited $9,000, $28,000, and $38,000 in our bank in a short period of time through our investments and were not paying any taxes on this money. We felt we were in the right field. And we were certain we could make a sizable income with investments (we had income coming from other properties at this time also). We quit teaching. We'd been cautious for long enough—now it was time to approach it as a career. And we've had no regrets.

At this point you need to make a change in the way you think. You need to take negative situations and turn them into profits for yourself.

When we began our business, interest rates were terribly high. Even the investors were discouraged. They were used to the seventies, when real estate was inflating like crazy! But we were just beginning our career and were excited about real estate. During this period there were very few other buyers out there, and we made some tremendous buys. We negotiated fixed rate owner financing on all of our first properties. It was a buyer's market.

Normally, on bleak, cloudy days when snow is on the ground, real estate shoppers are in front of the fire. But who do you think is out there tromping around in galoshes? You guessed it! A wonderful time to make low offers. Sellers are desperate!

I can remember an icy day last winter when we dragged our favorite realtor through twenty-four houses! The next day over a cup of coffee we wrote out ten offers. During the next few days we signed four contracts to buy. By our closing date the sun was out again and we had them fixed up, and we easily leased them during the spring.

The media is our best "boo bird." We love it when we hear those newscasts of doomsday in real estate! We love it because sellers hear them also. Remember, if you buy a home when people say homes are not selling, you're reversing that negative trend. And you're helping out a person who really needs to sell his home.

If you hear from a couple of realtors that a certain area is going downhill, turn the situation around. Real estate salesmen think they're doing their house-hunting clients a favor by keeping them away from areas going downhill, but that's not always true. Consider the other side of the coin. What are these real estate agents doing to the people trying to sell their homes? These sellers become very nervous—they know when real estate agents are warning people to stay away from their neighborhood. Who are they going to sell their homes to if salesmen will not bring people by to look at them?

They'll sell their homes to *you*. They'll be very grateful to see that one person who has the gumption to buck others' advice and buy homes in an "off limits" area. One day we went shopping in an area supposedly going downhill. We made many offers and bought four homes in that neighborhood. We lease-optioned all four of them for $10,000 to $15,000 higher than we paid. On top of this, they had $100 cash flow each. And we can pat ourselves on the back for what we did for the neighborhood. After word got out that four homes had sold, the area started looking up, and home owners felt more confident. Real estate salesman took a second look at the area. If homes are beginning to sell in an area, there must be a reason. If you, as an investor, moved into such a neighborhood, you might even help raise property values.

You can turn a downward tendency in an area around by going in and buying a few properties. Those houses may be run down but that can be changed. If you only buy a couple of homes, you want them all to be in neighborhoods that are thriving; that way you will not be in trouble when you want to sell. For those who are in the investment field to stay, however, it is a great feeling to lead the pack in turning an area around.

Of course you should still be able to feel safe and be able to go there after dark. We're talking of areas such as one next to an old shopping mall throwing in the towel, or a neighborhood that for some reason or another has had a setback. Who knows? Stay with real estate investing and you may just buy that old shopping center or theatre and really turn the area around.

The tendency for us had been to gradually begin to think big. By *think big* we mean that we now look at projects with more zeroes on the price tag. We're equally comfortable negotiating a package of thirteen duplexes as we are a $30,000 ranch. Of course, as you begin to think big you begin to hire a crew of people to help you with your work. No longer are you able to handle every aspect of the business by yourself.

We now hire many laborers to help with the clean-ups. We decided to relinquish toilet duty first! We usually swarm a house with a large crew of workers, and we direct traffic and handle the crises.

The next step for us has been to computerize our accounting system. Bookkeeping is very time consuming, but also very important.

We aren't sure where we're headed or how big we'll get, but we do know that as the wheels begin to roll, they turn faster and faster. Maybe we'll begin to buy commercial properties. Maybe we'll buy large apartment complexes. We know we love learning something new each day, and the challenges are endless!

You should have made a few choices by now; choices that will determine how, what, where, when, and why you will buy investment property.

If you want to supplement your income but don't want to spend a lot of time fixing up and managing your properties, consider looking for properties that are in good condition but are undervalued or whose owners are in a "must sell" situation. As an example, let's suppose you can find (and you may have to look quite a while) a house that should sell for $50,000. The owners have been transferred out of state (you figured that out from the phone number area code in the ad). They are making payments on a house they don't want and that they need desperately to sell.

When you find out that there is only one assumable loan on the property, for $39,000, you offer to assume the loan and give them $4,000 cash for their equity. They've had no luck selling and the payments are killing them, so they accept your offer. You immediately advertise the home, using every idea we've given you and a few of your own, and sell the house for $58,000 on a wraparound mortgage, with $5,000 down. The interest on the loan you assumed was 8½ percent, and you're charging twelve percent on the wraparound. Let's take a look at your profit:

> Your down payment $4,000
> The buyer's down payment $5,000
> Immediate income $1,000
>
> Your monthly payments $350
> The buyer's monthly payments $560
> Monthly income $210

You get every penny you invested back, plus $1,000 cash, and then you receive $210 a month until your mortgage is paid off, and $560 a month after that until the buyers pay off your wraparound mortgage (or pay off the balance in cash). The entire process took only a few weeks, *part-time*, and you have a good supplemental income . . . go out and do it again!

Don't be afraid to make many offers. We have made as many as ten in one day. They won't all be accepted. But if you don't make lots of offers, you can't expect to buy your quota of houses each month. So get out there and start negotiating!

If you're thinking that managing rental properties is the way to go, start looking for terms; for payments that are low enough so the rental income will pay for the property and give you a little monthly income as well. Structuring terms for positive rental income will be difficult with most properties. But if you know the rent you can charge for a property, work with the seller and try to come to agreeable terms.

If you love to fix up and decorate homes, and you have time (and a partner or two), you're really in luck. These are the homes with the best prices by far. The owners of a run-down home are usually eager to sell, and they already know they can't ask top dollar for their home. In some cases a sponge and warm, soapy water will bring the price of a home up by a thousand dollars. There is a tremendous potential for profit if you're handy with wallpaper and paint.

Only you can decide which avenue you want to follow in your investing. Part-time, full-time, buying and selling immediately, buying and renting, buying for equity growth, or tax shelter, or income . . . it's up to you.

Have you set any goals yet? If not, set them now. Don't wait for success, make it happen. You must be willing to work, to get out and buy real estate now.

It's unfortunate so many people who can grasp the possibilities easily can't find the strength and determination to persevere. If you're willing to work *and to stick to it*, you'll be amazed at how easy investing really is.

Get the word out. If you're serious about investing, let people know. Tell your friends and neighbors; have your husband (boyfriend, etc.) tell all of his friends.

One day a friend of Lynda's husband's who knew we bought houses told him he'd heard of a house in the suburbs priced at $36,000. He said the owner had called to say that he would accept $18,000 cash. Within the hour we'd purchased the house and two lots for $18,000. We still own the home, and the $350 rent makes the payments on the loan and gives us an additional $75 a month. The area is being rezoned for commercial use, and when we sell, it will be at a substantial profit.

Call every realtor in your area and introduce yourself. Let them know that you're serious, and if they find a deal that interests you, you won't hesitate to buy it. (Realtors hate wasting time with timid buyers—they're often happy to work with someone who can make a quick decision.)

One night, when Lynda was busy cooking dinner, a realtor called and told her about a listing that had come in that day. It was a three-bedroom house available for $23,000. Lynda told her to write up an offer on the spot, but the realtor said she wouldn't do that until Lynda had looked at the property. So

Lynda dropped her dinner and ran out the door. Within forty minutes she was back on the phone. She had seen the property and she wanted that offer written immediately.

We bought the home for $23,000, beating another offer by fifteen minutes! Our payments were $200 a month, and we rented it for a year at $350 a month. We sold it for $39,000. And all because we had put the word out that we were interested in real estate.

Have stationery and business cards designed. We've found that our advertising efforts pyramid over time. It may be a few months before word really spreads, but when it does, the phone never stops ringing.

Do you play the piano? If you play well, you think nothing of the fact that all ten fingers are flying up and down the keyboard, following a hundred black dots on a page. And yet the person looking over your shoulder—who can't play—is stunned. How could you possibly translate those marks into music, instantly? What's the difference? Experience and education . . . nothing more.

If you haven't invested in real estate, you'll find the entire process staggering: How could someone do something so complicated, and make it look so easy? Like the pianist, we have experience and education. And we have been willing to take the time, and put forth the effort, that success requires. Don't allow yourself to fall short. The entire world is waiting for you; don't wait another day.

CHAPTER THIRTEEN

Record Keeping

ORGANIZATION and accurate record keeping will make the difference between success and failure once you get your investing career rolling. Since you'll need to be highly organized a year (six months?) from now—when you're a professional investor—why not start now? Can you balance a checkbook? Don't worry if your answer is no; bookkeeping is an easily learned skill. If you haven't been a good record keeper before, we'll show you how to get started quickly and (relatively) painlessly.

The first thing to avoid is the tendency to throw all of your receipts and records into that big drawer by the fridge, waiting for a more opportune time to organize them. That time will probably come the day you can no longer slip another piece of paper into the drawer, and your organizing will probably consist of dumping them into a shoebox and stuffing it into a closet. If you already have such a drawer, and one or two such shoeboxes, just leave them where they are and start fresh with your real estate records.

The extra effort on a daily basis will pay off a million times, especially when your accountant is preparing your tax forms, or when the IRS decides it's time to audit your records. (No need to infuriate the tax man by dumping a box of receipts and old love letters into his lap.)

First thing: buy a filing cabinet and filing folders. An absolute must, these organizational tools will save you a hundred hours and a thousand gray hairs at the end of the year. You can buy file folders everywhere, from the local drug store to an office supply store. Label every folder, indicating what records are being stored there. You should also group the folders into sections—by month, or alphabetically, or by property, or in any other system you can think of. You need to put some thought into the organization of your files before you set up a system, and make sure that system will fit your plans. The idea is to set up files in such a way that you can put your fingers on any piece of paper you need within seconds.

Whenever you file something, write a brief explanation for future reference. When you throw the receipt for $48.12 into a folder in March, you know exactly what you bought; but come December 31 . . . good luck.

We keep a separate file on each property we buy, and in every rental property's folder we have an Activity Sheet on which we record *every* dealing we have with our tenants. Every time we talk to them, we make a note of the date, to whom we spoke, and what was said. You may find yourself in court one day, having to defend your actions. A record of every dealing with the other person will go a long way in persuading the judge that your side of the story has substance. If the plaintiff is a tenant you evicted, and he claims you never reminded him that he hadn't paid, your Activity Sheet—with a record of five phone calls and one visit—will stand up in court.

Record every inspection you make of your rental properties; make copies of every letter you send to tenants. In other words, do everything possible to document the fact that you have been a responsible landlord, and that any irresponsible actions that may have led to problems are the fault of your tenants.

Keep a record of rental payments. We do this on a piece of graph paper, with the addresses of our properties at the top and the months of the year along the side. We circle in red the months that we receive the rent late, and it makes for a striking graph, instantly pinpointing any problem tenants. You cannot leave such information to memory, especially when you own twenty properties around town. If you decide to evict a tenant for not taking care of the property and for paying late every month, you again have all the evidence you will need.

Keep a file that includes records of every banking transaction. Tellers do make mistakes—even thousand dollar mistakes—and the last thing you need is to find yourself digging frantically through a shoebox for the deposit slip that will prove you deposited $12,500 on May 12. Keep accurate checking account records, and file a bank reconciliation every month. (If you don't yet know how to prepare a reconciliation, wait a few pages and we'll explain the process.)

Another file is necessary for all closing documents. When you buy or sell a property, you'll receive several vital documents, and you cannot afford to misplace them. Disclosure statements, closing statements, trust deeds, contracts,

172

titles—every one of them is important. Keep the closing documents in each property's section of the filing cabinet, in a separate folder. Also keep a copy of every offer you make, even if it is not accepted. There's no sense in giving someone an opportunity to claim that you offered them something that you didn't.

The expense of maintaining and rehabilitating your properties is tax deductible, so you need to keep records of every dime spent doing these tasks. Record your mileage, money spent on supplies and labor, even the dinner tab for a business dinner spent talking about real estate (well, at least a portion of the dinner).

Ledgers

A ledger is nothing more than a piece of paper that somebody else has already divided into sections for you so you can organize your numbers. We use (and suggest) a 13-column ledger sheet like the one in Appendix C. We keep a ledger for our cash paid out and another one for income records. Let's look first at Cash Paid Out.

As you can see by looking at the example, we have devised a form that allows us to record every expenditure and to track those expenses to their sources. The form consists of two pages, so every penny spent can be recorded in the right column. There is a place for the check number, the date, and the amount of the check (this column allows for easy addition of all expenses).

We then record the expense in the category to which it applies. We always use our partnership money for expenses—never our personal money. If we must spend our own money, it is reimbursed out of partnership funds.

Not only do we keep track of where our money is going, we also love to track where it is coming from. To do this, we maintain a Recap of Deposits. We have provided columns for every source of income, and every dime that finds its way into our partnership also finds its way onto our deposit worksheet.

The next form is an absolute must: a bank reconciliation. If you file away your monthly checking statements from the bank (since they never agree with your register anyway), it's time you learned how to reconcile your account.

It's simple, really. All you need to do is take the balance your statement shows, add deposits you have made that don't appear on the statement, subtract the checks you've written that hadn't cleared the bank when the statement was printed, and you have an adjusted balance. Then subtract any bank charges from your register and you'll have another adjusted balance. If the adjusted balances agree, you have reconciled your statement. If they disagree . . . well, then somebody added wrong; you better check your figures again and make sure it wasn't you before you call the bank.

Our reconciliation does exactly this, as well as outlines all of the deposits and charges for easy reference. We take the balance per bank statement, add deposits not on the statement (in transit), subtract outstanding checks, and we have an adjusted balance.

We then take our balance at the beginning of the month, add all of the deposits made during the month, subtract all of the checks written, and voila! Our adjusted balance *always* agrees with the adjusted balance from the bank statement.

You should make a practice of preparing a reconciliation the day you receive your bank statement every month. Start now, on your personal account, and it will be a breeze when you're reconciling a business account.

We transfer our monthly income and expense record totals to an annual record. It allows us to see the flow of funds at a glance, and we can cut expenses and increase revenues easily with this vital tool.

Records, records, records. . . . We cannot emphasize enough the fact that accurate record keeping will make your life easier and your business more profitable. If you aren't handy with numbers, and if you can't find the power switch on a solar calculator, hire someone with bookkeeping skills. The price of competent help will be far less than a case of Tylenol at the end of the year.

CHAPTER FOURTEEN

Tax Incentives and Retirement Benefits

W E HAVE BRIEFLY MENTIONED tax incentives and retirement benefits throughout this book, but we haven't spelled out exactly how these jewels could line your pockets. It's important to understand this facet of your business.

We are not tax experts, not by any stretch of the imagination. But we've learned a few things about tax laws over the past three years, and we want to pass these very basic lessons on to you. Talk to your own accountant to clarify anything you do not understand, or that sounds too good to be true. You should have an idea what the tax laws are before buying any homes—considering tax consequences could lead you to structure your offers differently. So as you learn about real estate, pay attention to anything that refers to taxes.

Tempting Tax Tips

Nobody likes taxes, except an occasional accountant, and only a few people understand them. But they are not going to go away, and all we can do is try to pay as little tax as possible. This is one of the main reasons people buy investment properties.

Ask any accountant and he'll tell you that real property is possibly the best tax shelter: homes, land, apartments, and business buildings. Many accountants own real estate themselves; they do not like paying taxes any more than anybody else does.

Why are investment properties good for your taxes? There are several reasons. While any property you buy usually appreciates in value, the IRS approaches an investment such as real estate as an investment in material goods that will depreciate in value, like a car. Wear and tear, they assume, will make the value of your house go down. This, as we all know, is simply not the case. Talk to a person who bought a home twenty years ago and ask him how much the value of his home has gone down due to wear and tear on his property. He'll laugh and tell you that his house is now worth three or even four times what it was worth in 1965. As a rule, real property simply does *not* depreciate.

Another great reason for investing in real estate is that you deduct straight-line depreciation as an ordinary deduction (whether or not you itemize your deductions), and when you sell your property (if you have owned it for more than six months), only forty percent of the gain you realize from the sale is taxed as ordinary income. The sixty percent excluded from ordinary income is a tremendous break for the real estate investor.

Don't think the people at the IRS are dummies to allow people to take the depreciation deduction; they're fully aware that real estate does anything but depreciate these days. But they still approach real estate as a material good and allow you to use depreciation deductions. The tax shelter that real estate investing provides is a great attraction to people with money—it gets them to spend their money on homes they can rent to people who can't afford to buy property. Uncle Sam encourages people to invest their money this way; thus, the real estate tax laws have been created.

Capital Gains

One of the best inducements to buy real property lies in the capital gains tax law. This is the special tax on investment capital that allows you to pay taxes on only forty percent of the profits you make on the sale of your investment properties (if, as we've said, you own them for at least six months). If you're presently in the fifty percent tax bracket, you multiply forty percent times fifty percent to come up with what your profits will be taxed at—twenty percent. Obviously, with capital gains you're paying a much smaller tax on your profits.

The six-month capital gains holding period went into effect for investments purchased after June 22, 1984, but Congress is considering pushing that holding period back up to one year (where it was before) as of January 1, 1988. So now is definitely the time to start your investing career. By 1988, you could be rolling along, an old pro!

Deductions

You can also deduct quite a few items that go along with your investments. All of the interest paid on your homes—a hefty amount, especially the first few years you own those properties—is tax deductible. Let's consider a mythical house you bought for $50,000. We'll assume that the owner financed this sale and gave you a ten percent interest rate. You rent this house out for $500 a month to cover your mortgage payment. Of this mortgage payment you pay each month, you'll have to pay approximately $416 worth of interest. By the end of the year you'll be able to write off $5,000 worth of interest payments, no small amount. Although all this interest has been paid by someone else via rental income, the interest write-off is yours to put on *your* tax form because you own the property.

All of your property taxes are deductible also. The IRS does this because they realize that if they did not allow it, they would, in effect, be charging you a double tax on your property.

For those of you in an apartment now, but planning to buy a home, be aware that your interest payments and taxes on your personal residence are tax deductible too (we most fervently hope that those of you living in a home right now know this and knew it last April!).

The insurance payments you make on your investment homes are tax deductible also. (Just in case you're curious, a mortgage company requires that any property on which they make a loan has insurance. You must always have insurance—it would be too risky not to have it.) This insurance deduction is only valid on your income properties, not on your personal residence.

Any repairs and maintenance done on your property are deductible. If it costs you $2,000 to repair a roof on your income property, you can deduct this amount. We should make a clarification here: repair and maintenance work does *not* include an addition of a patio or a bedroom. An addition is an improvement, and improvements are not tax deductible, but must be depreciated over a period of time. Also, the labor for repair work you hire others to do is tax deductible, but if you do your own work on a home, your labor is *not* deductible. Yes, doing that work is costing you time, and your time is money, but the IRS is not willing to give us real estate investors everything.

All of your utility payments on income properties are deductible also. Your heat, water, electricity, sewer, trash removal, and air conditioning are all tax deductible. If, however, your tenant is paying for these things, they are not deductible.

As we have said before, all of the expenses and supply costs that pertain to your business—real estate investing—are tax deductible. This includes all of the mileage driven between income properties, your supply and equipment costs, any meals you have eaten while furthering your business (that coffee you drink at the diner while making an offer is tax deductible), all of your stationery, business cards—almost anything you pay for while pursuing your business is tax deductible. Of course, you'll have to retain proof that you did, indeed, buy all of these things; this is why we have told you to keep your receipts and keep it all organized.

(A note on your mileage and entertainment expenses while furthering your business: You must keep especially accurate and exact records of these expenditures or the IRS will disallow them. Spell everything out—the properties you go to on what day, the mileage involved, and what that meal you ate with a buyer was all about. Write down what type gas you prefer and what you had for dinner that night—you never know what kind of questions they might ask.)

Another deduction is the cost for maintaining your office. If you have an office outside your home, the rent or mortgage payments you make on it and all of your utilities are tax deductible. Even if you have an office in your personal residence, you can deduct some of your utility payments and part of your rent payment (if you are renting the place you presently call home). Your interest and taxes payment on your personal residence is already deducted and you cannot deduct it again because your office happens to be in your personal residence.

If you set up your office in your home, be aware that there are some sticky rules you must adhere to if you wish to deduct office expenses. There can be no bed or laundry hanging in your office—in other words, you cannot have it in your bedroom, a guest room, or a laundry room. It can't be your kids' playroom or where you make porcelain statues on the weekends. Your office in your home must be exclusively an office, and they will check this if you're ever audited. This office must be your *principle* place of business—as school teachers, we could not deduct the cost of heating our living room for grading papers, even if we did do some of our work at home. Also, you must actually make income with your office. If you claim to be a real estate investor and have your headquarters in your home, you must be making some money with your business. If you have not bought or sold a home since late 1977, it is doubtful you can deduct the cost of your office.

If you do have your office in your home, make sure to keep all of your utility and rent receipts, if you haven't done so in the past. Make copies of them and put them in your business tax deductibles file.

All of these deductions have made real property a good investment in the past, but in this decade there are even more reasons to get involved with property investments. In 1981, Congress first enacted the Economic Recovery Tax Act. This act was intended to induce people to buy and thereby help the economy. The act has been altered a bit, but it still basically says you can depreciate any properties purchased after March 15, 1984, as if it had only an eighteen year life.

Depreciation

This *eighteen year life* means that when you purchase a rental property, the IRS will look at the property as one suffering from unavoidable wear and tear for the next eighteen years, and consequently becoming less valuable. They will allow you to deduct the amount you paid for the property over that time period. As we said before, this "wear and tear" on your property will not be an unhappy factor; you'll be maintaining your property and watching it *appreciate* in value rather than depreciate. And you will have renters making monthly payments to you, covering your mortgage payments for as long as you own the property. Isn't this a marvelous gift our government has given us?

The only thing you cannot depreciate is the land that your structure—be it a home or an apartment complex—is sitting on. So allow a reasonable percentage of the purchase price for the land—get your CPA's advice on this.

Let's explain the above with some numbers. Supposing you buy a property for $50,000. The value of the land is twenty percent ($10,000), so you have $40,000 left which can be depreciated over the next eighteen years. You can approach this depreciation in two ways—you can use the straight-line method of depreciation or the accelerated method.

If you choose the straight line method, you can divide the purchase price by eighteen to figure your depreciation deduction for each full year that you own the property ($40,000 divided by 18 will give you $2,222). You can sub-tract from your income this amount of depreciation loss every year for as long as you own that rental property. To see how nice this deduction can be, suppose you own ten rental properties that you bought for $50,000 each—you would be able to deduct $22,220 from your taxable income!

Does this sound interesting? Well, the accelerated depreciation approach is even better for investors. It's a bit complicated but it will give you even more of a break come tax time, so make sure to ask your accountant about it—he can give you more detailed information than we can.

The accelerated approach gives you a table from which you determine what your deduction for depreciation will be—the number you take from this table to find your depreciation rate is determined by the month in which you bought your property. For example, if you bought your rental home in January, you would be allowed to take an eleven percent depreciation allowance for the first year. Using the $50,000 house as an example (with a structural value of $40,000), you could deduct eleven percent of the value of the structure (.11 x $40,000 =$4,400).

If you bought the property in February, you could deduct ten percent; in March, nine percent; and so on throughout the year. Obviously, your greatest savings are realized if you buy in January.

The difference between straight-line and accelerated depreciation becomes obvious when you sell the property. The accelerated method seems to be the obvious way to go, doesn't it? But if you have used the accelerated method on a rental property, the depreciation taken has exceeded the amount you would have taken on straight line, and the IRS will recapture the excess depreciation expense. Have your CPA review these tax consequences with you.

Which depreciation method you use is up to you, but you must use the same method every year you own the property, so don't fill out your tax forms the first year without carefully considering the consequences.

We realize how confusing taxes are; Taxspeak is a foreign language to all but the handful of people we call accountants. In fact, we call our accountant quite often, and you should do the same. Add a good accountant to your business team, and don't be afraid to ask questions—you are paying him to help you.

Net Operating Loss

Any business that has expenses in excess of revenues has a Net Operating Loss (NOL). The IRS is especially lenient with these losses; they allow you to deduct them from your income for the previous three years and/or the next fifteen years.

Don't get too concerned about these "losses." What the IRS sees as a loss and what actually happens to your bank account are two different things. Losses are your interest payments, taxes, depreciation, income-property, insurance fees, etc., to the extent that they exceed rental income. You can take NOLs backward when they add up to so much that they exceed your income for the year. You could be in this situation one day if you own enough properties.

With forty properties, for instance, assume that you "lose" $3,750 per year per rental—you will have a total of $150,000 worth of losses in one year. (Again, don't let that number upset you. Your renters have been paying these "losses" on each property for you.) Supposing you made a salary of $35,000 this year: You still have $115,000 worth of losses to use up—they are a proper deduction and you should never let it go to waste. So first, take it back and wipe out what you made three years ago. You only made $13,000 that year and did not pay much, but you'll still get your refund check. You're now down to $102,000 of losses. The next year you had to pay taxes on the same amount, so wipe out that $13,000 as well. Now we are down to $89,000 worth of losses. Last year was your first year of investing and you did it along with your old secretarial job—you made a total of $20,000 but weren't quite sure how to work this tax stuff so you didn't really try. Well, get rid of that income, too, and receive yet another tax refund from the IRS. You still have $69,000 left of losses—now take this forward and wipe out any money you may earn in the next fifteen years and pay less taxes then too.

Do you see why we like real estate investments so much? If we have purchased a property with none of our own money, we're claiming losses and depreciation that are not costing us anything—our tenants are paying for both of these while we receive the benefits of these tax laws. Can you think of any other investment that will allow you to do this?

There are other options that you have. You can trade a rental property with another investor who has a property he's willing to part with and the exchange can be tax free. The catch is that the properties you exchange must be of like kind—they must both be rental properties. You cannot trade a rental home for a residential home or a Ferrari. If you ever wish to do this, talk to your accountant and find out all he knows about it.

Retirement Benefits

One of the reasons we were so attracted to property investments was because of our concern about our retirements—we just don't trust the government to make sure that we live as well then as we do now. Real estate offers some very attractive retirement possibilities. You have probably begun to see these already, but we're going to draw them more clearly for you.

Suppose you buy a home now as an income property and put some renters in there so they make your mortgage payment for you. Let's assume that this investment home of yours is paid off in twenty years. Then your payments will be a thing of the past, your home is free and clear and in your hands, and you're still renting it out.

What is the rent payment you are receiving on this house? $400? $500? That money is coming in to you to put in the bank. Furthermore, $400 or $500 is what your home will bring in with today's rental market: Do you think rental prices are going to stay the same? They are not likely to. Think back twenty years ago: What were houses renting for back then? You will surely be able to charge more for rent in twenty years than you can today.

Suppose you bought five homes this year and rented them for the next twenty years. Your renters have paid your mortgage for you but you now own five properties free and clear and can put that money in the bank. If they all rent for $400 a month, you have $2,000 a month to play with, and you don't have to work for this money. If you own ten properties, you can reasonably double this amount. If you need some money in a hurry, you can sell or borrow on one of your properties. As you own it free and clear, you will be able to make quite a profit on it.

Do you think your social security check will match this? We're talking about very basic investments—think what you'll be worth if you own fifty properties by the time you're sixty-five. Or really use your imagination: suppose you get into advanced property investments and own three office buildings by the time you reach that age. The amount of money you receive for this could take you to Europe more than a few times. All of this is within your abilities.

Whether you go into investing in properties or not, make certain you own your own residence as you get older. There's a wonderful law that applies to your own home that you should know about. The house you actually live in will be exempted from any taxes on any profits up to $125,000 that are made due to appreciation if you sell it after you're fifty-five, even if you don't purchase another home. What this means is that if someone bought a home in 1964 at the age of thirty-six for $30,000 and today sells it for $150,000, all of that profit is excluded from taxes because this person is now fifty-six and the house made a $120,000 profit, which is under the $125,000 limit. Not bad, huh? You will be fifty-five sooner than you think (we know you don't like to think about it, and neither do we, but this doesn't mean it won't happen anyway). So own your own place of residence, and to really make things look nice once you feel like taking it easy, buy some other properties. With any extra money you have left over, you can send your grandkids to college.

In this chapter we have barely scratched the surface of all there is to be aware of as far as real estate tax and retirement benefits go. There's so much more to learn about real estate tax laws—volumes and volumes have been written on the subject. We don't expect you to read all these books, but get the advice of a person who has read most of them. We recommend you find an accountant who's well versed in real estate tax laws. Talk to him if you're feeling wary at this point. Let your accountant provide the tax alternatives to you. Remember what Lynda's accountant told her when she asked him about investing in rental properties: "You haven't got anything to lose!" You really don't, and there is so much to gain: a smaller income tax payment and more important, a secure future.

CHAPTER FIFTEEN

You Can Do It! (Self-confidence)

IF WE CAN, you can! We're certain that if you are willing to give the time we have to your investments, you can be as successful as we've been. We talked in the first chapters about the freedom an investing career offers a woman. What do you think, now that you have read the book? The three of us are happier and enjoy more freedom now than we ever had before. We spend time with our families that we simply could not before, because now we set our own schedules. If a crisis comes up at home, we can take care of it without having to call a boss and ask permission. The three of us are far better off financially than when we worked for someone else. We have the financial ability now to give our children a better future. We have money left over so we can take vacations. You can do the same!

You won't have to buy many houses to pay for your child's college bills, or your own education, if you're so inclined. By selling one house you bought as an especially good bargain, you could go back to school yourself! You could take off on that cruise you've never been able to take. We recently purchased one house specifically for cruising money.

It's so much easier to get out of bed in the morning when you enjoy what you do for a living. We jump out of bed earlier than we ever did before, just because the day ahead of us is exciting and the possibilities endless. We three have found our ultimate career, and we're very happy with it. We hope we have conveyed some of our enthusiasm to you.

We would like to see more women involved with income properties—it does so much for your self-confidence and self-esteem. You have an opportunity to challenge your brain as an investor! How much nicer we look to ourselves when that reflection in the mirror presents a successful person who is using her mind and creativity. We like ourselves better as investors than as school teachers; we feel we're not only using our potential, but we're getting paid handsomely for doing it. Many people, whatever their sex, are not living up to their potential, and this is a great shame. Any person should be the very best he or she can be and be happy with what he or she is doing. We feel that real estate investments can help you to be happier with yourself and more at ease financially. And if an investing career is not what you see as your ultimate career, it can at least make your ultimate career more feasible by giving you the required capital you need to get there. If you have secretly dreamed of opening a boutique in the shopping center near your house, you'll certainly be better prepared to do it. You will have acquired the knowledge to negotiate the lease. You'll be familiar with contracts and business problems. Real estate investing can be the answer to acquiring most anything you want.

While investing, you're affecting people and their lives. Do you have a job where you go home with a feeling of accomplishment, a feeling that you've done something worthwhile today? Can you actually see the results of your daily work?

It's a great feeling of achievement to change the face of a neighborhood that has been slipping downhill. Our new neighbors are overjoyed to see someone improving the street, and they sometimes offer to help us. We're improving their property values as we straighten up a neglected house, and they're glad it's happening. *This* is achievement—to improve a situation and be recognized for your efforts.

So many women are in jobs where their efforts are being totally ignored or taken for granted, which won't be the case with an investment career. What you're doing *is* being noticed, even by the local press and city government. We've had articles written about us in local papers and have been supported in our efforts by our city government. This certainly wasn't likely to happen to us in our teaching careers! We're contributing something to society and helping people by providing them with housing, something no one can do without.

It's also challenging to work the numbers to produce income and use our decorating talents as well. Even our conversations are now more invigorating, since we love to discuss our latest successful bargains.

Don't think we knew something special when we first started that you do not or cannot know now. When we started, in 1981, we were no different than anyone reading this book. We were not especially handy around the house—Carol had some fix-up talent, but she has learned much more since then. Now all of us are confident in our abilities to rehabilitate a house; we know what it takes to repair it and do much of the work ourselves when we choose to. We are equal to the challenge of making any property look like a winner for a small amount of money.

We didn't know much about real estate investing, either. The jargon that a realtor uses left us confused at first. But we learned and learned and learned through many hours of study. With each book we read, we felt more secure, more ready to go out and buy those first properties.

Do you think the average millionaire starts out differently? Of course, there are millionaires born into money, but their families had to get their money somewhere. Most of the richest families in this country have not always been rich. You'll find, if you check out a few books from the library, that somewhere in that now-rich family's background, an individual who dared to think differently, to take a risk, and reaped great rewards for doing it.

All self-made successes today do the same thing. They use their minds creatively, along with their knowledge, and stride forward, unafraid of trying something new—they *made* themselves successful. It takes determination and the ability to learn. You are just as capable of being a success as anyone else—you need to recognize this and let it motivate you. And keep in mind, most self-made millionaires used real estate as their means to success.

If you're nervous or cautious, don't underestimate yourself; everyone feels this way when he first starts—we certainly did. Anyone who tries something new is going to have certain fears, no matter who she is. But however inexperienced you are, if you are optimistic and determined, you won't fail.

We want to emphasize once again the importance of having a set of goals to follow. These are your blueprints for success. Don't wander around with vague ideas about what you would like to do with your investing career; vague ideas do not get results. Keep your "road map"—your goals—in mind at all times.

You're almost finished with this book. Are you going to close it, tell yourself that you'll do all this sometime, and then put the book on a shelf? Before you do that, we would like to remind you of just how far "sometime" is from now: it's related to never, and never is a long way from here. If the ideas you've read in this book sound interesting to you, do something about it! You can do something *today* that will get you moving on your career—read the ads! Take a walk and look at the houses around your home. What do you think they're worth? Would any of them make good investment properties? If you really feel ambitious, take a drive around. What about these properties? Do any of them look interesting at all? How many "For Sale" signs did you see?

If you're reading this at night, ask yourself what you will do tomorrow about what you have learned in this book. Write down your intentions.

Don't lose any enthusiasm that this book might have generated inside you. Let your enthusiasm loose! It is *not* too good to be true. If that means you march into a real estate office tomorrow and ask to see the MLS books, all the better! Go! Now there is all the reason in the world to get started with your investing career—every day that passes before you do something about it, is a day in which your enthusiasm wanes a bit more. If it wanes too much, you may have to read the book all over again! Or worse, you could lose interest in a career that could take you places you did not imagine.

For some of you this book could be the spark that ignites ideas that lead you to wealth. We hope so—we'd like to be partially responsible for such wonderful explosions of creativity and ingenuity. We'd like to see many women succeeding, as we have. We're one of the few female investing partnerships in our city, and, we'd like to see more women at our investors' meetings. Are you willing to come?

Act on your enthusiasm—take a chance and charge ahead of the others who are shaking their heads, clicking their tongues and saying that it can't be done. Ask them what they think after you have zeroed-out on your income tax and yet added to your income. Ask them (politely) if they still think it won't work after you have received your first profit on your first investment property.

Before we end this last chapter, we'd like to address a very sensitive issue, one we've had to deal with. It concerns the reputation that real estate investors have.

Once Lynda was asked a question by a very close friend that surprised her, but made her think. Her friend hesitantly asked, "Lynda, is what you're doing shady?" It was a shock to find that some people consider property investments to be more than a little on the other side of the law!

We would like to reassure you that no, most emphatically, *no*, there is nothing illegal about any aspect of real estate investments. This does not mean that everybody in real estate is running a legal business, but there are corrupt people in every field of business. With property investments, you can make a lot of money in a hurry—perhaps this makes people think there must be something shady about it.

No, there is not anything shady about investing in real estate. Only if you went looking for it could you find anything shady about it.

Our investments help people. We sometimes help people nobody else is willing to help. We once began watching a home that had been inherited by two teenagers after their father's death. As their father had actually died in the home, they did not enjoy being there at all. They had listed the house for sale with an agent, but the house wasn't attracting many prospective buyers. The poor kids did not know much about a home's upkeep—the house became messy and did not show well. No one was interested in buying it.

We went over there when we noticed the sign had fallen down. We talked to them, found that they desperately wanted out, and made an offer. With advice from some adults close to them, they accepted the offer. We bought the house. The kids, who had up until then been forgotten by the fast-moving adult world, had their needs taken care of. They moved into an apartment which was easier to maintain and not a constant reminder of the loss of their father. They're much happier now, with money coming in because of the sale and a new place from which to start their lives.

You can meet other people's needs with your investments and take burdens from their shoulders. The person who really needs to move because of a job transfer to another city is relieved when he talks to someone willing to help him. The couple who can no longer meet their mortgage payments are more than happy to talk to someone who will take their problems off their hands.

You're helping people with your investments in homes. You help owners who need to sell, renters who need housing, and buyers who need to find a home to live in. You're also boosting the economy by getting money in circulation.

Real estate may not be the most liquid, but it will always be one of the safest investments. People will always need a place to live. America is one of the most mobile societies in the world—we're a people who are on the move. There will always be people looking for a new home in a new city. You can provide this housing for them.

Whatever your situation, you can find a way to get into real estate investing. For some of you it could be more difficult, but it is possible.

We want to wish the best for you, and we hope that, like us, you'll be so excited by your new career that you'll wake up in the night with a new money-making idea that leaves you itching for morning so you can begin your plan.

Until we meet again—at an investors' meeting!

188

Appendix A: Real Estate Forms

This is an itemized check list for your property. This lists each item and its price individually so you'll know how your deposit is broken down. Your deposit will be refunded within two weeks after we receive possession minus any amount deducted from this check list.

1. All waterbed marks removed from carpet so no trace of its existence is left . . . . _____
2. All carpets to be thoroughly vacuumed . . . . _____
3. Any spots on carpets to be removed . . . . _____
4. Hardwood floors to be cleaned and polished . . . . _____
5. All mars and fingerprints on walls, in closets, and around light switches and plugs wiped away . . . . _____
6. Windows washed—sills dusted . . . . _____
7. Bathroom—tub &/or shower stall . . . . _____
      sink and vanity . . . . _____
      mirror and medicine cabinet . . . . _____
      floor . . . . _____
8. Linen closet . . . . _____
9. Kitchen—pantry, clean & washed out . . . . _____
      all cabinets, drawers, tile, & counter tops cleaned . . . . _____
      clean behind & under stove . . . . _____
      clean behind & under refrigerator . . . . _____
      carpet—remove any spots and clean if necessary . . . . _____
10. Basement—all debris removed, floor swept, dust removed from around furnace and top of hot water heater, cob webs removed from ceiling . . . . . . _____
11. Back porch cleaned . . . . _____
12. Garage cleaned and empty of all your debris . . . . _____
13. Sweep outside porch, steps, & walks . . . . _____
14. Lawn mowed & landscaping trimmed & flower beds cleared of weeds . . . . _____

LEASE AND OPTION TO PURCHASE REAL ESTATE

By this agreement made this _____ day of _____, 19____, between _____, hereinafter Lessor, and _____, hereinafter Lessee, Lessor leases to Lessee the premises located at _____ _____, together with all appurtenances, for a term of _____ months, commencing _____ and ending _____, at _____ o'clock ____.m.

• Section One •
Rent

Lessee agrees to pay, without demand, in advance, the sum of _____ _____ dollars, ($_____), per month for rent. Rent shall be due on the first day of each calendar month, beginning _____ 19____. Rent shall be delivered by hand or by mail to _____, or such other place Lessor may designate. Should rent not be paid in full within 5 days of the due date, Lessee shall be liable for a $25.00 late charge, payable at such time as the full rent is in fact paid. Lessee shall also pay $10.00 for each dishonored bank check.

• Section Two •
Security Deposit

Lessee shall deposit with Lessor, an amount equal to one month's rent as a security deposit. At the termination of this lease, Lessor may apply said deposit to accrued rent and any damages suffered by Lessor by reason of Lessee's non-compliance with the terms herein.

• Section Three •
Use of the Premises

The property shall be used as a single family residence, and occupied by ____ adults and ____ children under the age of 18 years. Lessee shall not allow an increase in the number of occupants of the property without written consent of the Lessor.

• Section Four •
Condition of Premises

Lessee stipulates that he has examined the premises and found the premises in good repair, and safe, clean and tenantable at this time, with the following exceptions: (see attached inventory if any)

1. _____

2. _____

3. _____

• Section Five •
Damage to Premises

If the premises are partially damaged without fault attributable to Lessee, his family, co-tenants, invitees, or agent, Lessor shall repair premises promptly. Lessor shall not be required to make any adjustments in the rent unless the premises are made untenantable by the damage.

Should damage to the premises result in the premises being untenantable, Lessor may terminate this lease and prorate any rent previously paid, or repair the premises and adjust the rent due according to the period of time the property remains untenantable.

• Section Six •
Maintenance and Repair

Lessee shall, during the term of this lease, at his sole expense, keep and maintain the premises in as good and sanitary condition as they presently exist. Lessee shall be responsible for repair of any damage caused by the neglect, negligence, misuse or waste of himself, his co-tenants, invitees, agent or guests. Lessee agrees to do the following:

1. Keep the yard and exterior in a clean, trim and picked up condition, water as needed to preserve landscaping, spray landscaping if needed to prevent infestation.
2. Remove from the dwelling unit and the premises all ashes, rubbish, garbage and other waste in a clean and safe manner.
3. Keep the plumbing fixtures in the dwelling unit as clean as their present condition.

4. Not engage in conduct or allow any person or pet to engage in any conduct that will disturb the quiet and peaceful enjoyment of others.
5. Keep the driveway and or garage free of oil deposits and automotive parts.
6. Change furnace filter regularly.
7. Keep weeds and dust from accumulating around air conditioning units.
8. Keep cats, dogs and all other animals away from the premises except as evidenced by the attached "pet rider."

• Section Seven •
Alterations and Improvements

Lessee shall make no alterations or improvements to the property without the written consent of the Lessor. All alterations and improvements made by the Lessee shall become the property of the Lessor, unless they are removable without damage to the property.

• Section Eight •
Dangerous Materials or Activities

Lessee shall not keep any substance, article or thing on the premises which might unduly increase the possibility of fire or explosion.

• Section Nine •
Utilities

Lessee shall be responsible for arranging for and paying for all utility services required on the premises, except that Lessor will provide the following utilities:

1. _____

2. _____

• Section Ten •
Right of Entry

Lessor shall at all times during the term of this lease, retain the right for himself or his agents to enter in and upon the premises for the purposes of inspection and for showing the property for lease and or sale. All entries by the Lessor or his agent shall be preceded by reasonable notice to the Lessee, except in cases of emergency to protect the premises from damage. Lessor shall also retain the right to place signs upon the property to aid in the sale or lease of the property.

• Section Eleven •
Abandonment

If Lessee, while in default of rent, shall be absent from the property for a period of seven (7) consecutive days, without first notifying and receiving approval from Lessor, Lessee shall at the option of the Lessor be deemed to have abandoned the premises. Should the Lessor deem the premises abandoned, he may enter the premises by any reasonable means and thereafter take possession of the premises and any personal property found therein. Lessor may re-let the premises immediately, and may charge and recover reasonable storage charges for storing Lessee's personal property. Lessor may attach and sell any personal property of the Lessee abandoned in the premises and apply the proceeds to accrued rent, storage charges, damages, costs of sale, or any combination thereof.

Recovery of the premises as set out above shall in no way alleviate the rental obligations of the Lessee under the terms of this lease. Lessor shall, however, be obligated to make reasonable efforts to mitigate his damages by reason of Lessee's default and abandonment.

• Section Twelve •
Default and Non-Compliance

If Lessee defaults in performance of any part of this lease, or fails to comply with any part or parts of this lease, the lease, at the sole option of the Lessor, shall terminate and be forfeited. If the Lessor decided to terminate the lease for any default other than non-payment of rent, he shall so indicate by written notice to the Lessee not less than thirty (30) days prior to the intended termination, stating the particular violation of the lease. Should Lessee cure the default or violation within fourteen (14) days of his receipt of notice, Lessor shall not terminate this Lease.

Termination and notices thereof for defaults in rent payment shall be effected pursuant to the Kansas Residential Landlord and Tenant Act, L.S.A. 58-2540 et. seq.

• Section Thirteen •
Assignment and Subletting

Lessee shall not assign this lease, or sublet or grant any concession or license to use the premises or any part thereof, without written permission of the Lessor. A consent by Lessor to one such assignment, sublease shall not be deemed a consent to any subsequent agreements. If a sublease is approved by Lessor, there will be a $75.00 fee to cover increased costs.

• Section Fourteen •
Notice

Any written notice required by this lease shall be deemed properly given when said notice is deposited by the sender, postage prepaid, to the receivor's address given in this document.

• Section Fifteen •
Insurance

Lessee acknowledges that Lessor has in effect insurance only for the structure and any insurance for the personal property and effects of the Lessee must be procured and paid for by the Lessee.

• Section Sixteen •
Hold Harmless

As part of consideration in this agreement, Lessee has agreed and does agree to hold Lessor harmless on any claims made against Lessor by any third party claiming injury and or damages as a result of being in or on the premises.

• Section Seventeen •
Possession

Lessor shall deliver possession of the premises on or before the commencement of the term of this lease. Should Lessor not deliver possession within 5 days of said commencement, Lessee may terminate this lease, but in no event shall Lessor be liable for any damages claimed or sustained by Lessee by reason of his failure to deliver possession at said commencement.

• Section Eighteen •
Receipt

Lessor acknowledges receipt from Lessee of the following sums as of the date of this agreement:

1. Partial month rent _____
2. Full month rent _____
3. Security deposit _____
4. Pet deposit _____

   Total received _____

If this agreement is not signed by Lessor within 5 days of receipt of this money, or Lessee properly terminates this agreement under Section Seventeen, the receipted funds shall be returnable in full to Lessee no later than 14 days from the date Lessee signs this lease, all by demand of Lessee. Should Lessee not take possession or otherwise indicate that he does not desire to fulfill this agreement subsequent to paying the above monies, but before commencement of the term, Lessor shall be allowed to keep the receipted funds if notified of Lessee's intended breach more than three (3) days following the execution of this document.

• Section Nineteen •
Manager

The Lessee is hereby notified that the Manager and the Landlord are as follows:

Owner: _____

_____

Agent for service: _____

_____

_____

Mail check to: _____

_____

_____

OPTION TO PURCHASE

Lessee shall have the option to purchase the leased property at any time during the lease period for a price of $_____. Such option shall be exercisable by Lessee only if Lessee is not in default of the lease at the time of exercising this option. Such option shall be exercised by the Lessee by written notice to the Lessor not less than ninety (90) days before the end of the lease period. If such option is exercised, Lessor and Lessee shall, within 10 days after such exercise, execute and acknowledge in duplicate the contract of sale attached to this lease as Exhibit A.

As consideration for said option to purchase, Lessee shall pay to Lessor the sum of $_____ payable at the execution of this agreement, receipt of which is hereby acknowledged by Lessor. If said option to purchase is not exercised by Lessee, said sum shall not be returned to Lessee by Lessor without interest at the termination of this lease.

As additional consideration for said option to purchase, Lessee shall pay to Lessor the sum of $_____ per month payable on the first day of each month, which sum shall not be returned to Lessee if the option to purchase is not exercised.

Should the parties not desire to include an option to purchase in this lease agreement they shall so indicate where allowed on this document.

WAIVER OF OPTION

The Lessor and Lessee acknowledge by their signatures below that they do not intend to include the option to purchase section of this lease.

_____   _____

Lessee   Lessor

The parties acknowledge that they have read this lease agreement and that all of the terms and conditions have been explained to their satisfaction. This lease agreement shall be binding on the heirs and assigns of the parties hereto.

_____   _____

Lessee   Lessor

B 119—Notice to Tenant, 3 Days, English and
Spanish; public assistance statement: 10-83

© 1983 BY JULIUS BLUMBERG, INC.
PUBLISHER, NYC 10013

Notice to Tenant
Aviso al Inquilo

To: .... 19........
A:

The sum of *La suma de* $ ....

for rent from *para renta de* .... 19........
to *a* .... 19........

Tenant of the above premises:

TAKE NOTICE That you are justly indebted to the Landlord of the above described premises as set forth above, which you are required to pay on or before the expiration of three days from the day of the service of this Notice, or surrender up the possession of said premises to the Landlord, in default of which the Landlord will commence summary proceedings under the Statute to recover the possession thereof.

Inquilino del local arriba mencionado:

TOME AVISO: Que usted adeuda al casero de la propiedad arriba mencionada según lo arriba expuesto que usted debe pagar en o antes del término de tres dias a partir del dia que usted reciba este aviso o entregar posesión de dicho local al casero. En caso de incumplimiento el casero comenzará un juicio sumario de acuerdo a la ley para recobrar su propiedad.

.... Landlord, *Casero*

.... Agent, *Agente*

Immediately, if you are currently receiving public assistance, bring this three-day notice for rent to the worker who handles your case. Your worker will consider this notice on an emergency basis and may be able to provide funds to avoid the possible loss of your apartment.

If you are not currently receiving public assistance and require financial help, you should apply immediately at your local Income Maintenance Center. If you show this notice to the receptionist, you may also be entitled to assistance on an emergency basis.

Inmediatamente, si esta recibiendo asistencia pública al presente, traiga este aviso para pagar renta dentro de tres días al trabajador que maneja su caso. Su trabajador considerará este aviso con carácter de emergencia y posiblemente podrá proveerle fondos para evitar que usted pierda su apartamento.

Si no recibe asistencia pública al presente y necesita ayuda financiera, usted debe solicitarla inmediatamente en su centro local de mantenimiento de ingreso. Si muestra este aviso a la recepcionista, usted posiblemente podrá tener derecho a recibir ayuda con carácter de emergencia.

Notice to Tenant

Landlord

Tenant

State of New York, County of   ss.:   SERVICE OTHER THAN BY PERSONAL DELIVERY

being duly sworn, deposes and says, that deponent is

over 18 years of age and resides at No.

Deponent was unable to serve   tenant by personal delivery

The property described in the within notice is No.

On the   day of   19   at   o'clock   M. deponent served the within notice

strike out inapplicable statements

SUBSTITUTED SERVICE — by gaining admittance to said property and delivering to and leaving a copy thereof personally with a person of suitable age and discretion, who was willing to receive same and who — resided — was employed — at said property

CONSPICUOUS PLACE SERVICE
☐ by affixing a copy thereof upon a conspicuous part, to wit: — the entrance door   of said property;
☐ by placing a copy thereof under the entrance door of such premises;
deponent was unable to gain admittance thereat or to find a person of suitable age and discretion willing to receive same.

MAILING — and within 1 day thereafter, on   19   by mailing a copy thereof enclosed in a postpaid properly addressed wrapper to respondent at the property sought to be recovered which is respondent's residence or corporate respondent's principal office or principal place of business by registered-certified-mail and by regular first class mail.

use either (a) or (b) if applicable
(a) which is individual tenant's last — residence address — place of business or employment address
(b) which is corporate tenant's last known principal office or principal place of business within the state by depositing the same in — a post office — official depository under the exclusive care and custody of the United States Postal Service within the state.

Sworn to before me on

....
The name signed must be printed beneath

STATE OF NEW YORK, COUNTY OF   ss.:

being duly sworn, deposes and says: deponent is over 18 years of age and

resides at

On   19   deponent served the within notice

Check Applicable Box

☐ Affidavit of Service By Mail — (a) on   tenant of premises No.

by depositing a true copy of same enclosed in a post-paid properly addressed wrapper, in — a post office — official depository under the exclusive care and custody of the United States Postal Service within the State of New York.

☐ Affidavit of Personal Service on Individual — (b) on   tenant of premises No.

by delivering a true copy thereof to the tenant personally. Deponent knew the person so served to be the person mentioned and described in said notice as the tenant therein.

Deponent describes the individual served as follows:

☐ Male	☐ White Skin	☐ Black Hair		☐ 14-20 Yrs.	☐ Under 5'	☐ Under 100 Lbs.
☐ Female	☐ Black Skin	☐ Brown Hair	☐ Red Hair	☐ 21-35 Yrs.	☐ 5'0" - 5'3"	☐ 100-130 Lbs.
	☐ Yellow Skin	☐ Blond Hair	☐ Balding	☐ 36-50 Yrs.	☐ 5'4" - 5'8"	☐ 131-160 Lbs.
	☐ Brown Skin	☐ Gray Hair		☐ 51-65 Yrs.	☐ 5'9" - 6'0"	☐ 161-200 Lbs.
	☐ Red Skin	☐ White Hair		☐ Over 65	☐ Over 6'	☐ Over 200 Lbs.

Other identifying features:

☐ Affidavit of Personal Service on Corporation — (c) on   a corporation, tenant

of premises No.

by delivering a true copy thereof personally to   an officer

of said corporation: deponent knew said corporation so served to be the corporation described therein as tenant and knew said individual to be the   thereof.

Sworn to before me on

....
The name signed must be printed beneath

PET DAMAGE DEPOSIT
LEASE AGREEMENT RIDER

Landlord hereby grants lessee permission to have a pet (_____) in the premises. A $ _____ damage deposit has been deposited by lessee as a security for damages to the premises incurred by such pet. All pets must be cleared by the landlord before being accepted. This deposit shall not limit lessee's liability for damages caused by such pet or pets in excess of the amount of this deposit. Dated this _____ day of _____, 19___.

LANDLORD: _____

LESSEE: _____

Appendix B: Needs Questionnaire

1. Do I want to add to my income monthly?
2. Could I be happy with a chunk of money every six months instead of a monthly income?
3. Is my first need a retirement plan and peace of mind later in life?
4. Could I produce an income by tax savings alone?
5. Do I want to be a landlord?
6. Am I looking for a career change?
7. Will I need to schedule my investments around my present job?
8. Do I have the strength and desire to rehabilitate a piece of property?
9. How many hours a day or a week do I want to devote to my new venture?
10. Will my family be supportive of my new venture?
11. How much risk am I willing to take?
12. Could I benefit from a partner?
13. Does my credit rating limit my purchasing ability?
14. What are my strong points? My weak areas?
15. What members do I need on my team—accountant, attorney, handyman, real estate agent, etc.?

Appendix C: Ledger Samples

National® 45-613 Eye-Ease®
  Brand   45-713 20/20 Buff
          Made in USA

Cash Paid Out: _____For Month of _____, 19___

Ck. #/	Date/	To Whom	Amount	Mortgage Payments	Utilities	Materials	Contract Labor
1							
2							
3							
4							
5							
6							
7							
8							
9							
10							
11							
12							
13							
14							
15							
16							
17							
18							
19							
20							
21							
22							
23							
24							
25							
26							
27							
28							
29							
30							
31							
32							
33							
34							
35							
36							
37							
38							
39							
40							

6	7	8	9	10	11
pairs	Office Supplies	Advertising	Insurance	Appliances	Taxes

WEALTHY WOMEN

National® 45-613 Eye-Ease®
45-713 20/20 Buff
Made in USA

Cash Paid Out: _____ For Month of _____, 19__

Ck. #/ Date/ To Whom	Amount	Earnest Deposits	Accountant & Legal	Bank Service Charge	Salary: Jane
1					
2					
3					
4					
5					
6					
7					
8					
9					
10					
11					
12					
13					
14					
15					
16					
17					
18					
19					
20					
21					
22					
23					
24					
25					
26					
27					
28					
29					
30					
31					
32					
33					
34					
35					
36					
37					
38					
39					
40					

6	7	8	9	10	11
alary: ynda	Salary: Carol	Loan Proceeds	Closing Transfers	Security Deposits	Other

Glossary

Accelerated Cost Recovery: A method of deducting the cost of a property investment from income taxes over an eighteen-year life, with more deductions in the first years of owning it.

Amortization: The process of paying off a loan with equal monthly payments over a period of years.

Amortization Schedule: A small book or a computer printout that lists monthly payments on various loan amounts at different interest rates and over different periods of time. This is one of the most important items an investor can have.

Appraisal: An estimate or opinion of value on any material good.

Appreciation: The increase in value of a material good due to economic fluctuations.

Assessment: A charge or lien against a property, usually by a city or county government, for work that was done for the property: a new sidewalk, improvement of sewers, etc.

Assets: Everything that a person owns that has value, cash, jewelry, real property, cars, stocks, etc. The more assets a person has, the better.

Assumption: The process of taking over another person's loan for a home and the payments.

Auction: Where the sale of property to the public takes place.

Balloon Payment: The final payment of a loan—this payment is usually larger than the previous payments.

Bill of Sale: A legal document that transfers a property title to another party.

Capital: Money. Cash. Or, if you prefer, financial reserves.

Capital Gain: Any increase in value of real property over a certain amount of time (now it is six months). The seller of this property may claim a special reduced tax after he sells it.

Cash Flow: The spendable income after all bills have been paid for any period of time, usually a month. Cash flow can be positive, meaning there is some money left over, or negative, meaning there isn't. "Negative cash flow" is synonymous with "change your strategy."

Closing Statement: A statement given to the buyer and the seller at a closing of a property that details the amounts of money involved in the transaction.

Commission: A fee paid—usually seven percent of the sale price—given to a third party who helped sell or rent a property. Your real estate agent's paycheck.

Contingency: A condition listed in a contract that must be fulfilled before the contract is valid.

Contract: An agreement on paper between two or more parties who agree to perform certain duties. In real estate, it is the paper on which you make your offers to buy houses.

Conventional Financing: A loan from a bank, financing company, mortgage company, savings and loan, etc., without the federal government's involvement.

Co-signer: A person who signs any legal document (contract, mortgage, etc.), taking on equal responsibility for the performance of duties contained in that document.

Deed: A written, legal document that gives title to a property.

Deposit: An amount of money given upon the agreement to buy or lease a property—it is a guarantee to the seller or leaser of the buyer or lessee's good intentions.

Depreciation: Loss in value of a material good for any reason.

Discount Points: A loan fee charged by a lender. Either a buyer or a seller may pay these points.

Earnest Money: Related to a deposit, this is given to a seller as proof that a person making an offer on a property intends to carry through with the purchase of the property. Always ask for some sort of receipt if you give one of these to a seller.

Equity: The value of real estate outside of all amounts owed—loans. The money an owner has tied up in his property.

Escrow: An account for all money and documents with a third party (this third party does not necessarily have to be a person—for example, it can be the account that holds funds for a partnership) that complies with the wishes of the involved parties.

Exercise Option: When a tenant who has gotten into a property with a lease option goes ahead and buys the home.

Fair Market Value: What a house will go for on the market—this amount is determined by appraisers.

FHA: Federal Housing Administration.

Finder's Fee: A fee paid by a seller to someone who helped him find a buyer for his property.

Gross Earnings: Total profits in any field before deducting operating costs.

Industrial Bank: A lender that has lots of money, usually available at higher interest rates than at regular banks.

Lease: An agreement via contract between the owner of a property and one who would like to rent it.

Legal Description: A formal description of the location of real property that is recognized by law.

Lessee: Leasee. The person who rents a property.

Lessor: Leaser. The landlord who is renting the property to another.

Leverage: The process of using the money already invested in properties to buy more properties.

Liabilities: Any debts for which a person is responsible, or any claims against a corporation or individual.

Lien: Any claim against a property.

Listing: A contract giving a third party the right to sell or lease a piece of property.

Loan Value: The amount determined by an appraiser that sets the money required from a new mortgage.

Mechanical Inspection: An inspection by a qualified individual that ascertains whether a house's electrical, plumbing, heating and cooling systems are in good working order.

MLS: An abbreviation for Multiple Listing Service, an organization that publishes listings in weekly books.

Mortgage: A loan with real property as the security backing it up—if the payments are not kept up, the property can be taken over by the mortgagee.

Mortgage Banker: A person who deals in mortgages.

Mortgagee: The person lending money—giving the mortgage.

Mortgagor: The person borrowing the money—taking the mortgage.

Net Worth: The difference between a person's assets and her liabilities. How much money a person has to play with.

Notice to Pay Rent or Quit: A notice to a renter that he must make his rent payment or leave the property. This notice is required by law in most states before a tenant can be evicted.

Points: One percent of the total loan—this amount is usually given to the lender as a fee when loan is given.

Prepayment Penalty: A charge against a person who borrowed money if he pays off the loan before the loan was to be fully paid. Always check on these before signing any papers.

Principal: The amount of money that is outside of interest or profits. In a loan, the amount that one is actually paying for the property, as opposed to the interest.

Promissory Note: A written contract or note that promises to pay a certain amount at a certain future time.

Realtor: Any real estate broker or agent who is a member of the National Association of Real Estate Boards.

Redemption: When an original owner takes his property back after foreclosure—he can only do this if he pays the back payments on it. An owner is given a certain period of time to do this after the auction of his house. This time period varies from state to state.

Second Mortgage: Loans given with a certain property offered as security for the loan. There can also be third and fourth (or any number within reason and the value of a property) against a property.

Straight Line Depreciation: As opposed to Accelerated Cost Recovery, this entails dividing the cost of your home by the depreciation life (eighteen years presently). This amount can then be deducted from your income taxes each year.

Sublet: When a tenant rents the property he is leasing to another party.

Subordination Clause: A clause that benefits the borrower—the lender releases his priority to a following mortgage or trust deed.

Tax Penalty: A charge against a property owner for not paying his taxes on time.

Title: Proof of ownership of any valuable.

Trust Deed: A form of mortgage—a loan. Three people are involved with a trust deed: the trustor (person borrowing the money), the trustee (person holding title until the trust deed is paid off—usually a county's Public Trustee), and the beneficiary (the lender).

VA: Veteran's Administration.

Zoning: How a piece of property may be used, as determined by city, county, or state governments.